At ✵ Issue

Indian Gaming

Stuart A. Kallen, *Book Editor*

Bruce Glassman, *Vice President*
Bonnie Szumski, *Publisher*
Helen Cothran, *Managing Editor*

GREENHAVEN PRESS
An imprint of Thomson Gale, a part of The Thomson Corporation

Detroit • New York • San Francisco • San Diego • New Haven, Conn.
Waterville, Maine • London • Munich

For more information, contact
Greenhaven Press
27500 Drake Rd.
Farmington Hills, MI 48331-3535
Or you can visit our Internet site at http://www.gale.com

LIBRARY OF CONGRESS CATALOGING-IN-PUBLICATION DATA
Indian gaming / Stuart A. Kallen, book editor.

p. cm. — (At issue)
Includes bibliographical references and index.
ISBN 0-7377-2388-2 (lib. bdg. : alk. paper) —
ISBN 0-7377-2389-0 (pbk. : alk. paper)
 1. Gambling on Indian reservations—North America. 2. Indians of North America—Gambling. 3. Indians of North America—Economic conditions. 4. Indians of North America—Social conditions. I. Kallen, Stuart A., 1955– .
II. At issue (San Diego, Calif.)
E98.G18.I529 2006
363.4'2'08997—dc22   2005040263

Contents

Introduction

Until the late 1980s the only legal casinos in the United States were located throughout the state of Nevada and in Atlantic City, New Jersey. In 1988, however, Nevada and New Jersey lost their gambling monopolies as a result of a Supreme Court decision concerning the Cabazon Band of Mission Indians who live on a reservation in the Coachella Valley near Palm Springs, California. The Court ruled that California's antigambling laws do not apply to Indians because Indian reservations are regulated by federal, not state laws. Although the ruling concerns a specific California case, as a matter of federal law it applies to all states whose laws prevented Native American tribes from running gambling operations.

After the ruling, state governors and attorneys general asked their congressional representatives to pass federal legislation regulating gambling on reservations. The result was the 1989 Indian Gaming Regulatory Act (IGRA). According to Laura Hansen Smith in *The Tribes and the States*, the IGRA has three purposes: "[to] provide a statutory foundation for Indian gambling operations as a means of promoting economic development, self-sufficiency, and strong tribal government; to prevent the infiltration of organized crime and other corrupting influences; and to establish federal regulatory authority, federal standards, and a National Indian Gaming Commission."

Antigambling groups strongly opposed the IGRA, which allows Indians to open casinos in states where gambling, in many cases, had been illegal since the nineteenth century. Supporters of the bill, however, believed that the IGRA would help the millions of Native Americans who were among the poorest people in the United States. Those living on reservations suffered high rates of unemployment, poverty, child mortality, suicide, and alcoholism. As Anthony Pico, chairman of the Viejas Indian tribe in California told interviewers for the PBS show *Frontline* in 1997:

> Before gaming and revenue our people lived in despair, in abject and grinding poverty. . . . Do you

5

know what it feels like to see your people living in despair and the reality for them is alcoholism? Do you know what it feels like to be able to have to ask others for the basic necessities of life for food? . . . [This] lifestyle was not a choice that we made. Our people were driven into arid areas. We were driven into the mountains, into the rocks. [We] languished there for . . . 200 years not having an opportunity to access the economics of this rich and abundant country.

Few could argue with Pico's assertions. However, when the Indian Gaming Regulatory Act was written, lawmakers did not foresee the unintended consequences and wide array of complex problems that would result. The first noticeable effect of the IGRA was a rapid growth in the numbers of casinos operating in the United States. They made a total of $5 billion profit on $12.7 billion revenue in 2002 alone. Their success, however, has created a host of disputes between gaming operators, citizens, and state, city, and county governments.

One of the greatest controversies concerns sovereignty, the unique status that distinguishes Native Americans from other Americans. The precedent of tribal sovereignty was set in the seventeenth and eighteenth centuries by the British, who negotiated treaties with Indians that acknowledged the tribes as independent, or sovereign, nations. After the United States won independence from Great Britain in 1783, this policy was enshrined in the U.S. Constitution, which refers to tribes as being separate entities from the states. Article III, Section 8, Clause 3, of the Constitution states: "The Congress shall have the power to regulate commerce with foreign nations and among the several States and with the Indian tribes."

As sovereign entities, tribes make and enforce their own laws on reservations, provide services for citizens, raise and spend revenues, regulate commerce, establish citizenship rules, and negotiate with other state and local governments. The tribes, however, have no legal obligation to work with local governments where casinos are located, raising questions about whether tribes, as sovereign nations, have to adhere to zoning and environmental ordinances, tax and labor laws, and other regulations.

As the courts try to resolve the complex legal issues concerning sovereignty, non-Indians who live near palatial, glitzy casinos say they have suffered while a few tribe members have profited enormously. Foxwoods Resort Casino, run by a small band of Pequot Indians in Ledyard, Connecticut, is a prime example. The casino is the largest in the world, with 320,000 square feet of gaming space in a 4.7-million-square-foot complex visited by sixty thousand people every day. Author Kim Isaac Eisler describes problems created by Foxwoods in *Revenge of the Pequots: How a Small Native American Tribe Created the World's Most Profitable Casino:*

> Noise and exhaust from buses were now the norm in what was once one of the most rural and quiet corners in America. . . . By 1995, Route 2 [leading to the casino] . . . was a constant rumble of buses and cars crammed with boisterous out-of-towners. . . . Suddenly in what had been one of the quietest patches of America, crimes were being committed that had been unheard of in the past.

While the casino radically changed the neighborhood, Foxwoods boosters point out that the casino created twelve thousand jobs in a region with traditionally high unemployment. And in a special agreement with the state, the casino pays Connecticut a 25 percent tax on its slot machine revenue every year—over $200 million in 2003. This is more than the taxes paid by United Technologies Corporation, a high-tech aerospace company that is the state's largest employer. In addition, the casino paid more than $400 million in taxes and fees to the federal government.

Indian gaming supporters also point out that successful tribes have used their casino revenues to build houses, schools, roads, and sewer and water systems. Tribes also fund clinics, health care, and education for their members while ending their historical dependence on welfare and charity. However, critics say that while some tribes have provided benefits for members in Connecticut, California, Minnesota, Florida, and other areas with successful casinos, the majority of Native Americans have not profited from the casino boom. About 175 casinos located in rural, unpopulated areas are barely profitable. Another 350 Indian nations do not participate in gaming, and the needs of their tribe members are as great as ever on reservations where unemployment can be as high as 85 percent. In the 2002 article "Wheel of Misfortune" in *Time* magazine, Donald L. Barlett and James B. Steele explain:

Revenue from gaming is so lopsided that Indian casinos in five states with almost half the Native American population—Montana, Nevada, North Dakota, Oklahoma and South Dakota—account for less than 3% of all casino proceeds. On average, they produce the equivalent of about $400 in revenue per Indian. Meanwhile, casinos in California, Connecticut and Florida—states with only 3% of the Indian population—haul in 44% of all revenue, an average of $100,000 per Indian. In California, the casino run by the San Manuel Band of Mission Indians pulls in well over $100 million a year. That's about $900,000 per member.

The problems of tribal casinos and the casino's effects on poverty, sovereignty, race relations and society are debated in *At Issue: Indian Gaming*. The authors present differing, often competing, opinions on property rights, government regulation, casino-related crime, and the historic rights of Indians in the modern United States. With billions of dollars pouring into Indian gaming coffers every year, the controversies surrounding casinos will probably remain contentious for some time to come.

1

Gaming Provides Many Benefits to Native American Communities

Walking Antelope

Walking Antelope is a member of the Coeur d'Alene tribe, located in the northern panhandle of Idaho. He maintains a Web site devoted to Native American issues and hosts an Internet radio show that features Native American music.

Although critics of Indian gaming claim that casinos cause crime and drain the finances of local governments, studies have shown that these charges are unfounded. While there are some problems associated with Indian casinos, funds from the operations have helped some tribes achieve unprecedented independence and prosperity in a short time. Indian gaming might not solve the problems of all Native Americans, but for the first time in centuries, tribes have been given a chance to compete and succeed in the economy of the United States.

Indian gaming in America has become a multi-billion dollar industry, which many Tribes have embraced as a tool to pull their people out of poverty and unemployment. A multitude of benefits have become possible through gaming, both for the Tribes and the neighboring communities, but it has also created many problems for the very people it was meant to help. Despite the side effects, casino gambling continues to supply the tribes with much needed income. Large-scale Indian gaming has been around since at least 1978, with the first unregulated appearance of bingo halls on Indian reservations. This was ten years before congress passed the Indian Gaming Regulatory Act (IGRA) and establish[ed] the National Indian Gaming Commission (NIGC) to regulate the rapidly expanding tribal gaming industry.

> // *There is no definitive link between gambling and bankruptcy.* //

Side effects of Indian gaming have been varied: problems in the home, loss of income from bankruptcies [at]tributed to gambling, and suicides resulting from gambling losses and addictions. Also cited are higher crime rates, as compulsive gamblers seek more funds to continue gambling. Political and religious speakers also insist that Indian Gaming is basically "immoral". Opponents contend that through Indian gaming tribal members reap huge profits in America, yet they do not pay taxes. One myth that this writer has heard from an opponent to gaming stated: "Tribal gaming drains resources and tax dollars from surrounding non-Indian governments, and communities."

In an April 27, 2000, a US General Accounting office (GAO) report by Frank Wolf, Congressman and avid gambling opponent from Virginia, found that there is no definitive link between gambling and bankruptcy. The report continued announcing that systems to track family problems, crime and suicide generally do not report the reasons for these incidents, "so they cannot be linked to gambling".

Treating Problem Gamblers

The Tribal gaming organizations do recognize and contribute to treating compulsive gamblers. Charles Flowers of the Knight-Ridder/Tribune Business News reported in an article the following:

> Besides requiring stiffer regulations, including background checks on casino employees, tribal gaming administrators also scored higher than Las Vegas or Atlantic City when it came to recognizing and treat-

ing compulsive gamblers. Tribal casinos averaged 18 referrals of either customers or employees for treatment last year, compared to 4 referrals by top-25 non-tribal casinos, and 9 by non-tribal casinos below the top 25.

Tribal casinos are doing a much better job in treating the problem gamblers than the gambling industry as a whole. The same Knight-Ridder article reveals that the Mashantucket Pequot tribe contributes $200,000 annually to the Connecticut Council on Compulsive Gambling.

In northern Idaho, the Nez Perce Tribe & Casino funded the creation of a Gambling Support group. This group was formed in March of 2001. The first order of business of the 8–10 members attending the meetings was to vote all connection with the casino/tribe out. The very people it helps now supply all costs. They meet every Saturday, at Saint Joseph's Regional Medical Center.

> *This huge industry creates a large tax base, in the associated payroll taxes, and employee income taxes. Almost all goods and services required by Indian casinos are obtained locally.*

Sherman Alexie, Coeur d'Alene author and poet, addressed the morality of Indian Gaming. "How immoral is the Washington [or Idaho] State Lottery? How immoral are the beer and tobacco companies?" As with many other services, there is a demand (for gambling), and Native Americans partially supply that demand.

Improving the Economy

Contrary to the popular myth, Indian people pay all taxes required by state and federal government. They pay federal income, FICA and social security taxes. Only a small percentage of Indians who live and work on their perspective reservations are not required to pay state or property taxes. Communities have benefited by the opening of casinos in their neighborhood. In example the Coeur d'Alene Tribe of Idaho donated

$949,000 to local schools and libraries in [fiscal year] 2000.

According to a report by Jonathan Taylor of Harvard University, "Indian casinos have substantial beneficial and economic and social impacts on surrounding communities." Two other key points were presented: "No evidence of harmful economic or social impacts due to Indian casinos' introduction is discernible in 30 indicators of economic and social health." And on the crime issue: "Our data indicates that communities witnessing the introduction of a proximate Indian casino experience a substantial net decline in auto theft and robbery."

> **❝** The buffalo . . . [once] gave . . . Indians everything they needed to survive and prosper, so now in the 21st century Native Americans turn to the gaming industry as their means of survival. **❞**

Indian Gaming is an 8.6 billion dollar a year industry according to figures from the Director of Research, Katherine Spilde, Ph.D., of the National Indian Gaming Commission. It has created a large number of jobs in the communities where gaming has appeared, over 200,000 as reported in 1999. Non-Indians hold approximately 75% of all jobs in the industry. This huge industry creates a large tax base, in the associated payroll taxes, and employee income taxes. Almost all goods and services required by Indian casinos are obtained locally. Again adding to the benefits of the local governments and communities.

The Indian Nations sought out new revenue sources and a way to benefit their people. They found it through gaming. They did this after decades of poverty, unemployment, and high mortality rates for adults and infants. . . .

There are limited economic opportunities on most reservations. Reservations were created on land that had very little use to anyone except the tribes, and they had no say in where their reservations were located. They are for the most part rural, and on land with little or no tax base. It was an area not wanted by the general public. As the result of poor economic prospects in agricultural, mining and forestry, gaming is the only industry that is viable on many reservations.

With decades of reduced government funding and very

limited alternatives the Native American Tribes were forced to find other avenues of economic advancement. Out of a total of 558 federally recognized tribes 198 are engaged in gaming operations. Indian gaming comprises only 10% of the total American Gambling Industry. But this small part receives the lion's share of attention by the opponents of gaming. Most of this opposition is from the states that have their own form of gaming: lotteries, bingo, card rooms, horse and dog racing, pull-tabs and full fledge casinos. Competition is those states' main concern, not social [and] economic problems associated with gaming.

Despite all the growing pains associated with this fledgling industry, it continues to benefit the Native American communities. Gaming on today's Indian reservations is a necessary venture to gain independence and prosperity for a people long at an economic disadvantage. Many tribal leaders believe gaming should only be a stepping-stone to further economic advancement, and on many reservations that is the case. Indian gaming is not the right path for all the tribes, but for those that have taken that step, it is a powerful tool to acquire self-determination and self-reliance. The buffalo before the great slaughter of the late 1800's gave the plains Indians everything they needed to survive and prosper, so now in the 21st century Native Americans turn to the gaming industry as their means of survival, their way to prosperity.

2

Most Native Americans Have Not Profited from Gaming

Jacob Coin

Jacob Coin is executive director of the California Nations Indian Gaming Association (CNIGA), an association of more than fifty Indian nations in the state. Prior to his work at CNIGA, Coin was executive director of the National Indian Gaming Association (NIGA) in Washington, D.C. He is a member of the Hopi Indian tribe, Tobacco clan, from the village of Kykotmovi in Arizona.

Native Americans have endured many stereotypes over the past centuries but perhaps the most ironic is that of the "rich Indian." It is true that a small percentage of the nation's Indians have benefited financially from the gaming boom. However, most of the 2 million Native Americans in the United States live below the federal poverty level. Like many other stereotypes, the myth of the rich Indian has had harmful consequences. It is used by politicians who want to balance state budgets by cutting programs that benefit impoverished Native Americans. The term "rich Indian" is also used disparagingly by those who resent the recent success of Indian gaming. While fighting poverty and hopelessness, Native Americans must also fight false images of the rich Indian promulgated by politicians, media sources, and others who should know better.

A lot has been written about the "myth of the rich Indian," the mistaken notion that tribal government gaming has eliminated poverty and neglect in Indian country. While the benefits of tribal gaming are evident in the 28 states where some 220 tribes operate 330 casino and bingo operations, prosperity has not trickled down to most Native Americans. Tribal government gaming generated $14.5 billion in revenues in 2002, but just 41 of the operations won 65 percent of the gross. Roughly 20 percent of tribal casinos are generating 80 percent of the revenues.

Most tribal casinos and bingo halls are marginal operations providing valuable jobs and economic development on Indian lands. But they are not creating untold riches. Of course, if you were to stack all the newspaper articles written about the lucrative Foxwoods Resort in Connecticut [owned by the Pequot tribe] it would tower over what has been published about all the other 329 tribal gaming operations in the United States. The result is the misconception that all Indians are rich Indians.

This myth of the rich Indian has created some tragic consequences in California. As a result of a deepening budget deficit [in 2004] Gov. Arnold Schwarzenegger and the state Legislature [proposed making] some drastic cuts in state and local services to needy American Indians. Local American Indian tribes could see the end of a new experiment in managing their own welfare programs. Elected officials are proposing to slash by 70 percent ($30.5 million from $43 million) funding to the Temporary Assistance to Needy Family [TANF] program being administered by the California Tribal TANF Programs. In addition, state and local funding for substance abuse and alcohol prevention at Indian health clinics has been slashed from $2.8 million to $100,000, virtually wiping out the program.

> *Most tribal casinos and bingo halls are marginal operations providing valuable jobs and economic development on Indian lands. But they are not creating untold riches.*

"The non-Indian community believes that because of the success of gaming tribes there is no need to provide services to indigent Indians living in California," says Marilyn Delgado, tribal liaison, California Tribal TANF Partnerships. "What people do not realize is that most of the 300,000 Indians in California are not members of California tribes. Many are members of tribes not recognized by the federal government. Others are members of tribes that are not significantly benefiting from gaming. "The state of California has the responsibility to provide for all needy people, including Indian people who reside within the state," Delgado said. "Furthermore, it is not the responsibility of gaming tribes to provide for needy Indians who are not members of their tribe."

> *Much of the Yurok reservation is without essential services such as water and electricity. Many tribal members live below the poverty level.*

Tribal leaders are coordinating to petition the governor not to cut the funding, Dennis Turner, project director for the tribal welfare program in San Diego County, told the *North County Times* newspaper. "We need to work with the governor's office and that's what's happening," Turner said.

State Cuts Would Hurt Impoverished Indians

Tribal welfare is a $90 million program that receives about half of its funding from the state. It receives $46 million from the federal government. However, losing $30 million from the state could spell doom for the fledgling programs, Delgado said.

Until 1996, needy tribal members had to look to county government to access welfare programs, which were often far from the remote Indian reservations. Under federal welfare reforms that took effect in 1996, tribes were allowed to administer their own programs, thus taking them off local governments' hands. Tribal officials have said the change allowed greater spending flexibility and the ability to provide local services.

H.D. Palmer, a spokesman at the state's Department of Finance, told the newspaper the cuts are being proposed because of a "declining tribal case load" in welfare rolls. He added that the state would continue to fund tribal welfare and that the program would continue to receive federal money. "There is still revenue through state and local programs," Palmer said. "They will still be receiving federal funding."

A Misguided Policy

Meanwhile, Gov. Schwarzenegger is calling for California gaming tribes to rewrite portions of tribal-state gaming compacts agreed to in 1999. He wants a greater share of tribal gaming revenues to help bail the state out of its fiscal woes. The governor singled out Indians in the October [2003] recall election that swept him into office, claiming tribes did not pay "their fair share.". . .

If the governor's team believes all California Indians are rich Indians, the talks [between tribes and the governor's negotiating team] may be a learning process.

As is the case nationally, much of the publicly surrounding tribal government gaming in California centers on the larger, more lucrative operations. . . . But there are some 54 tribal government casinos in the Golden State, and only 15 have the maximum 2,000 machines as allowed in the tribal-state compacts. There are between 40,000 and 50,000 enrolled members of the state's 107 federally recognized tribes. And more than 6,000 of them are members of just two tribes, the Hoopa Valley and Yurok tribes in Northern California. Hoopa Valley has fewer than 350 machines. Yurok has no machines at all. Hoopa Valley is still struggling with some 40 percent unemployment. Much of the Yurok reservation is without essential services such as water and electricity. Many tribal members live below the poverty level.

As California Nations Indian Gaming Association Chairman Anthony Miranda suggested in his landmark speech in January [2004], the contributions of tribal gaming to the economic well being of American Indians and their non-Indian neighbors has been "nothing short of spectacular." But tribes in California and throughout the country have a long way to go before they achieve economic and social parity with their non-Indian neighbors. And, as Miranda also pointed out, it must be done without compromising basic principles of sovereignty and self-governance.

The prospects of us all becoming rich Indians will likely remain a myth. But we can secure for our children, and the generations to come, a secure and bright future.

3

Casinos Help Indians Achieve the American Dream

J. David Tovey Jr.

J. David Tovey Jr. is the executive director of the Coquille Indian Tribe and the former executive director of the Confederated Tribes of the Umatilla Indian Reservation in Oregon. He is the president of the Affiliated Tribes of Northwest Indians Economic Development Corporation in Shoreline, Washington, and was named Oregon's Economic Development Leader of the Year in 2001.

The tribes of the Pacific Northwest have built flourishing gaming facilities while maintaining honesty, professionalism, and integrity. Their success has allowed associated tribe members to have financial security, decent health care, and improved schools. While there have been some genuine problems with the explosive growth of tribal casinos, most tribes have behaved honorably. At long last, Indians of the Pacific Northwest are able to participate in the American ideal of life, liberty, and the pursuit of happiness.

In response to William Safire's Dec. 15 [2002] column addressing Indian gaming ("Non-Indians Benefit Most from Casinos."), the tribes in the Pacific Northwest invite readers' scrutiny. We have come to believe that our tribes are approaching the gambling industry much as we have our other governance and resource responsibilities—with caution, with respect and with great honor.

It's rather easy to dismiss one's honor when speaking in terms of millions of dollars. But the American people have to realize that Indian people feel as though we've been through this before—when the values of the external society felt driven to take lands in westward expansion and later to take our great Columbia River and its abundant salmon. Many of our elders warned us that our success would attract unwanted attention from those who will covet our newfound prosperity and influence.

The Northwest tribes believe we are "textbook examples" of how to ethically move into the lucrative gambling industry. We feel as though we were very cautious before entering the industry. Most tribes did not jump into gaming but began developing gaming resources over five years after the Indian Gaming Regulatory Act. In my tribe's case, the Confederated Umatilla Tribes in northeast Oregon, we surveyed our members, reservation residents and non-tribal citizens of our bordering community of Pendleton.

> *Our elders warned us that our success would attract unwanted attention from those who will covet our newfound prosperity and influence.*

We received a mandate of nearly two-thirds of all populations to move forward with gaming. Since then, our services and employment have multiplied, making us a respected government and the second-largest employer in a rural, economically depressed area of Oregon. We have, in effect, a job for every tribal member who chooses to have it, and jobs for hundreds of non-Indians who live nearby. We're proud that we are offering family wage jobs with one of the best benefits packages in our area.

Establishing Our Own Solutions

Safire so easily dismisses the National Indian Gaming Commission [NIGC] as the sole guardian of safety, security and integrity of Indian gaming, yet he entirely overlooked our capable local tribal gaming commissions, our own law enforcement agencies, NIGC's federal partners (FBI, the IRS, the U.S. Treasury), our teams of accountants and auditors, some of the most so-phisticated surveillance systems around and, at least in Oregon, a whole division within the Oregon State Police—funded entirely by tribal assessments from our gaming revenues.

> *Organized crime really didn't frighten you, but organized Indians seem to.*

We very much took to heart the industry's adage to have people watching people watching people. A cash business simply requires these safeguards. We challenge any other industry or jurisdiction to match our systems. So, please, spare us the old argument of anything like a "level playing field" with regard to our reservations and businesses. As history has shown time and time again, it is not level and never has been.

Indeed, the entire tone of Safire's column harkens to the paternalistic days when local, white communities all the way up to Congress felt the need to "solve the Indian problem." The reality is that tribes have been successful in their ventures only when we have ultimately planned and established our own solutions. After 150-plus years of failed federal government stewardship, the suggestion that these failures somehow gives the ill informed the right to condemn our current advances, I feel, reflects a fear of college-educated, economically independent Indians. One gets the sense that some would like us to be confined to remote reservations and dance for the occasional tourist. Organized crime really didn't frighten you, but organized Indians seem to.

Safire has chosen to examine only the wealthiest and poorest of our 500-plus tribes nationwide. I'm quite certain any research confined to the extremes would point out inefficiencies and inequities, be it [in] education, health care, business, government or religion. The true story resides nearer the center of the bell curve where the majority of our gaming tribes are making fundamental improvements to their entire system of services, programs, businesses and governance.

Instead of the allusions of corruption, many tribes are enjoying unparalleled prosperity, a renewed sense of community and open expectations of hope and improvement for the future—something that was not made available under 200 years of federal government policy. These successes, under any other name, would be nothing short of a Renaissance of Indian Country.

We in the Northwest have a saying, "Indian Country: Where the American Dream Began." For 200 years, Indians have not been part of this American economic miracle. But, like the immigrant parents and grandparents of all of your readers, we Indians are finally tasting the fabled American Dream. As a result, be assured, we are here to stay.

4

Casino Riches Have Been Managed Wisely by the Choctaw

WBUR

WBUR is a noncommercial FM radio station licensed to Boston University. As a member station of the Corporation for Public Broadcasting, WBUR has won more than one hundred awards for its news coverage.

The wealth provided by Indian gaming has created problems on some reservations where unequal distribution of profits and questionable business practices have caused disputes. In Mississippi, however, the Choctaw have been able to avoid these problems by wisely managing the profits from their gaming operations. Instead of handing out monthly checks, the Choctaw are using their earnings to guarantee jobs and schooling and to preserve their language and culture. They are also investing in nongaming businesses. The Choctaw have used their gaming windfall to benefit all members of their tribe.

The controversy swirling around issues of tribal legitimacy and behemoth casinos [such as the Foxwoods Resort Casino] in Connecticut obscures examples elsewhere of quiet success with tribal gambling. The Mississippi Band of the Choctaw Indians are a case in point. [In 2002] the tribe opened its second casino, the Golden Moon, in Philadelphia, Mississippi. It's smaller than the billion-dollar facilities in Connecticut. Still, the 9,000 members

WBUR.org, "The Casino Where Everybody Wins," www.wbur.org, 2003. Copyright © 2003 by WBUR.org. Reproduced by permission.

of the Choctaws clear $100 million a year and the casino represents the latest step in a stunning Indian renaissance.

Two generations ago, the Choctaws were the poorest tribe in the poorest state in the nation. Fergus Bordewich, author of "Killing the White Man's Indian," spent time on the Choctaw reservation in the 1960s, when it was "a forgotten community; just a scattered collection of cabins and shacks in a depressing corner of the Mississippi backcountry." Bordewich recalls that the reservation's roads were unpaved, kids were unclothed, and most of the tribe was far removed from the world of money and jobs.

John Hendrix, a non-Indian who works in the tribe's economic development office, says at that time just 7 percent of the tribe had high school educations; 86 percent earned less than $2,000 a year. "To see where we are today," says Hendrix. "really paints the picture of what has been done in a short amount of time."

Tribal Leadership and Talent

The story of the Choctaw renaissance is the story of tribal leadership and of the talents of Chief Phillip Martin, who has led this tribe for most of the past 45 years. Martin is a short, stocky man with slicked-down black hair and a down-to-earth style that seems at odds with the tribal powerhouse he's built. As a young soldier in post-war Germany he was inspired by Europe's determination to rebuild its shattered continent. And he felt the same was possible for the Choctaws, most of whom lived in dirt-floor shacks and depended on government welfare. "It's just not a good way to live," Chief Martin says matter-of-factly.

> *There's enough work for every member to have two jobs, and the tribe also provides thousands of jobs for non-Indians.*

So Martin went to work. With the help of the Great Society Programs of the 1960s [that provided economic and educational assistance] the Choctaws built an industrial park and became the first Indian tribe to compete aggressively for low-skill manufacturing jobs, and it worked. They went into business with General Motors to assemble components for trucks and cars. More business followed: a factory that makes automobile speakers for Ford and Chrysler, a direct mail business and a construction firm, for-profit nursing care, a company that makes plastic knives and forks for MacDonald's, and since 1994—casinos. Today the 9,000-member tribe is fully employed; in fact there's enough work for every member to have two jobs, and the tribe also provides thousands of jobs for non-Indians.

The Region's Economic Engine

The Golden Moon casino is a long, curved, orange edifice—topped with an enormous glittering sphere that houses a restaurant and lounge—and looks like a giant golf ball ready to tumble down onto the fountains below. If not beautiful, it is impressive. And its amenities have brought something new to this once sleepy edge of east Mississippi.

Jim Prince, publisher of the *Nashoba Democrat* newspaper, remembers when the Choctaws were known as an impoverished tribe, plagued by chronic unemployment and alcoholism. Today they represent the region's economic engine, with golf courses, water parks, and casinos. "People here aren't really used to that," says Prince, who recalls opening day at the Golden Moon with the awe of a small boy catching his first glimpse of a fire engine. "People still go out and marvel that this is in the red clay hills of Nashoba County; seems like you're somewhere else—not here."

A few local residents from the town of Philadelphia complain about the increased traffic and worry about being swallowed up by the casino. But for the most part, the non-Indian community embraces what the Choctaws and the man everybody here knows simply as "Chief" are doing. They're grateful for the jobs and the economic vitality it has brought to this county. David Vowell, who heads a local community development group in town, says Chief Martin has always made an effort to give back to the off-reservation community. "He's offered to help with the local park, the local library," according to Vowell, who adds, "People ask for money and he writes them a check."

Once known for racial division and the murders of civil rights workers in 1964, Philadelphia, Mississippi, is now known for its prosperous tribe that has brought whites, blacks, and Indians together. Town-tribe relations are clearly better here than in Connecticut. Choctaws sit on local boards and work closely with town officials and lines of communication are open. Chief Phillip Martin says another key difference is that the Choctaws have always been here. "And we look like Indians," he adds with a mischievous smile in his eye.

The Casino Does Not Define the Tribe

This is a tribe with a casino, as opposed to a casino that defines a tribe. In the casino there are no tribal icons or other reminders that this is an Indian enterprise. The Choctaws say this is their business, not their culture. And the tribe's John Hendrix says the casino is just one part of a broad economic strategy that follows years of success with low wage, low profit enterprises. "It's important that we had that experience before the casino," says Hendrix. "When we got the revenue from the casino we knew how to use it."

> *[Chief Phillip Martin has] offered to help with the local park, the local library . . . people ask for money and he writes them a check.*

The Choctaws don't get cash stipends; they are guaranteed jobs and college educations. And profits from the gambling is plowed back into other business ventures as well as tribal housing, schools and roads. "I look at it this way," says Chief Martin, "it's how you use the proceeds from the gaming, and I believe we're using them the right way."

Not everybody across the state is a fan. For example Sam Begley, who represents Mississippi's non-Indian Gulf coast casinos, says it's unfair that the Choctaws don't pay state taxes. "We pay 12 percent of gross revenues in taxes, which is a disadvantage," he says. Begley says the Choctaws are having it both ways: on the one hand, he says, they are governmental and sovereign, but on the other, private and entrepreneurial. "There is a fairness issue," he says. "All businesses want to be treated the same."

Begley accepts the idea that Indian tribes deserve a helping hand, but he argues that with [the] advent of the Civil Rights act, the Fair Housing act, and the array of government assistance programs, there ought to be some way to break the back of racial disadvantage that stops short of giving special privileges and advantages to a particular group. "I would like to think," says Begley, "that the Choctaws want to be a part of our country."

> *" The Choctaws are . . . using their casino wealth to preserve their native language, which is still widely spoken on the reservation by tribal elders. "*

For their part, the Choctaws argue they don't pay state taxes because they don't get state services. The tribe pays for its own police and fire protection, court system, and roads. And Chief Martin says there's good reason that federal law protects reservations from the reach of state tax-collectors. "If there's something to be gotten from the Indian, [the states] usually get it," says Martin. "Congress was wise," he adds, "that the state would want to get its hands into the tribal coffer, and so it didn't allow that."

New Wealth, Old Customs

The Choctaws are also using their casino wealth to preserve their native language, which is still widely spoken on the reservation by tribal elders. The fear of some on the reservation is that as this tribe becomes further integrated into mainstream America, the younger generations will lose their linguistic roots. Now, with the new wealth generated by the casino, Rossana Tubi-Niki has been able to establish a Choctaw language program. "In the past I've harped about the need for such a program," says Tubi-Niki, "but the problem has always been that we didn't have the money."

Now the Choctaws do, so the language instruction begins in the reservation's Head Start program, where tribal elders like Lula May Lewis, introduces Choctaw to the tribe's youngest members. Speaking through an interpreter, Ms. Lewis says she cherishes the language and is happy to be ensuring that it lives on.

On the day of my visit to the Head Start Center, a small boom-box in the corner of the room was playing traditional Choctaw dance songs. When I trained my microphone on it,

Lula May Lewis approached and began to sing along. It turned out that long before she became a language teacher, she was a tribal singer. It was an interesting moment: the modern boom-box in harmony with the tribal elder, which prompted a discussion with Rossana Tubi-Niki and her assistant, Jesse Ben, about the effect of all this wealth on the tribe; about using casinos to preserve tribal traditions.

Both of them were pleased about how the wealth has helped the tribe, but they also had some reservations. "My concern is when do we slow down?" asked Jesse Ben, who is worried about how progress can also be the enemy of tradition. Rossana Tubi-Niki agreed; she said since the casino opened, many tribal members are choosing to work two jobs. "I can see family values and spiritual values going down the drain," she says. It was a strange moment in an otherwise positive conversation about the benefits of tribal wealth and the preservation of cultural traditions. But as Ms. Tubi-Niki put it, "too much of anything can go bad."

As problems go, too much affluence is a pretty good one to have. And it's one that a generation ago no tribe in this country could even dream about.

Contemporary Indian law is animated by the goal of restorative justice; that the country owes something to Indian tribes as recompense for its brutal policies of the past. But what does it owe? Economic opportunity? Special rights? Casinos? The issue is complicated by the collision of two powerful forces: the reach of Indian sovereignty and the explosion of casino gambling across the country. Given the corrosive power of money and politics, it's not surprising that the idea of nations within nations has led to confrontation and cynicism about Indian rights in places like Connecticut. But not everywhere. The Mississippi Choctaws used their sovereign power, including their casinos to pull themselves and many of their non-Indian neighbors out of poverty and out of isolation from each other. Taken together, these stories might point to a need for review and reform of federal Indian policy; but they also demonstrate the benefits of effective Indian leadership in America.

5

Sudden Casino Wealth Has Both Benefited and Harmed California's Chumash Tribe

Glenn F. Bunting

Glenn F. Bunting is a staff writer for the Los Angeles Times.

Until the 1990s, people on the Chumash reservation in Southern California lived in dire poverty, many without electricity, steady employment, or hope. The legalization of Indian gaming, however, drastically changed life for members of that small tribe. Today, the Chumash are among the wealthiest Americans. Many own several homes, luxury automobiles, and are able to take vacations to exotic locales. Although this sudden wealth has created its own problems, it has served as partial reparation for the destruction of the Chumash by California's early settlers. While nothing could ever compensate the Chumash for the pain suffered by their ancestors, the profits from Indian gaming will allow the Chumash to preserve their culture and provide for their tribe members for many years to come.

Growing up on the reservation, Kenneth Kahn waited in line with his mother for brick cheese, powdered milk and other government surplus food. He does not have a college degree or a paying job.

Glenn F. Bunting, "A Life of Payouts, Not Handouts," *Los Angeles Times*, November 8, 2004. Copyright © 2004 by the *Los Angeles Times*. Reproduced by permission.

Yet at 27, he has accumulated more wealth than many working Americans will see in a lifetime. Every month, Kahn receives a check for nearly $30,000—his share of profits from the Chumash Casino Resort [in Southern California].

Scattered in his yard on the reservation here are a silver Range Rover, two oversized pickup trucks, a high-powered speedboat and a pair of all-terrain vehicles. He owns a vacation home in Lake Tahoe and recently paid $1.6 million for a five-acre estate in Santa Ynez.

"People ask me if I think I deserve it," says Kahn, his shiny, dark hair neatly bundled in a ponytail.

"Not more than my ancestors," is his standard reply. "I don't care how many casinos we build," he says. "We could never overcome what was taken from our ancestors."

A Torrent of Money

For much of the past two centuries, the Chumash of Santa Ynez lived in anonymity and abject poverty. As recently as the 1960s, reservation homes lacked running water, electricity and phone service. A decade ago, some Chumash still relied on welfare and donated clothing.

Then came the casino.

Since 2000, when California voters granted Native American tribes the exclusive right to offer Las Vegas-style gambling, each of the 153 members of the Santa Ynez band has received more than $1 million in casino income.

The torrent of money has caused a jarring transformation in the life of the Chumash. It has provided financial security and a bounty of material goods. It has enabled the Chumash to revive their language and instruct their children in the tribe's ancient traditions.

But the sudden riches also have sparked conflict and fevered spending. Some tribal leaders worry that the monthly casino check is simply a new form of dependency, as corrosive as the welfare payments of old.

In the decades before gambling, many Chumash Indians toiled as ranch hands, truckers, maids and farmworkers. Now, they hire day laborers to tend their own sprawling estates.

They play golf at country clubs and vacation in Paris, Madrid and Maui. So many tribal members own vacation property in the Sierra Nevada that they jokingly call the area "Chumash North."

Members who once subsisted on rice and beans enjoy

gourmet meals and expensive bottles of champagne at their own upscale restaurant, the Willows. Women who once wore hand-me-downs and turquoise beads wear precious jewels and have cosmetic surgery.

"We're not standing in line anymore to get cheese," says Julio Carrillo, 60, a member of the tribe. "It's like the American dream. . . . We got ours."

> **❝** I don't care how many casinos we build. . . . We could never overcome what was taken from our ancestors. **❞**

Gambling proceeds pay for free medical care at a modern Chumash clinic and subsidize private schooling, tutors and college tuition.

And a people who had been relegated to the margins of history are reclaiming their identity. A decade ago, the tribe—formally the Santa Ynez Band of Mission Indians—had been largely assimilated into the local Latino community. Many were ashamed to acknowledge their Native American ancestry.

Now, casino earnings are underwriting efforts to build a Chumash museum, scour European collections for Chumash artifacts and revive the Chumash Inezeño language.

Powerless for so long, the Chumash are asserting their sovereign rights with new vigor, aided by lawyers, lobbyists and consultants.

"Given the way we were raised, we could never have imagined what we have today," says tribal chairman Vincent Armenta.

The Downside of Instant Wealth

Yet the costs of newfound wealth are as striking as the luxury cars that ply reservation streets and the private pools that dot backyards.

Some of the Chumash have run through their riches, spending themselves back into debt. So many people have gotten overextended that the band has withheld money from members' monthly checks to pay overdue car loans and taxes.

The casino money has ignited bruising internal battles over

ancestry. Some tribal members are challenging the bloodlines of their fellow Chumash, contending that they lack the one-fourth Indian blood required for enrollment in the band.

The money has also added to the bitterness of marital breakups. With legal support from the band, several Chumash Indians have fought to prevent former spouses from collecting casino money as part of divorce settlements, arguing that the tribe, as a sovereign nation, is exempt from California's community property laws.

But the Chumash don't dwell on the downside of instant wealth.

Kenneth Kahn, for one, sees only progress. Growing up, he was barely aware of the world beyond the reservation. Going away to college never occurred to him.

"My mom worked two jobs. I never saw her," Kahn says. "If I had any direction, it would have been a different deal."

Today, Kahn makes sure his 7-year-old son, Austin, has opportunities he didn't. The boy attends a private Christian academy, is assisted by a tutor and attends after-school and summer programs—all made possible by the casino.

Last year, Kahn was elected to the five-member business council that runs the tribal government. "I'm not proud of getting money for doing nothing," he says. "I want to do the best I can to earn it."

He is taking classes in political science and communications at Santa Barbara Community College and is thinking of pursuing a four-year degree.

Years ago, Kahn's grandmother, Rosa Pace, led the effort to bring drinking water, medical care and other basic services to the reservation.

Yet Pace, now 75, feels a deep ambivalence about the wealth generated by the casino. She is among a group of Chumash elders who call themselves "guilty Jag owners."

Pace still washes dishes by hand and only recently yielded to relatives' demands that she have a garbage disposal installed.

"It's difficult," she sighed. "I do feel guilty."

Ancient Tradition

Historians say that Chumash Indians have maintained a continuous presence in Southern California for at least 5,000 years.

The earliest recorded sighting by a European was in October 1542, when Spanish explorer Juan Rodriguez Cabrillo encountered Indians in wood-plank canoes along the Santa Barbara and Ventura County coastline.

The Chumash were expert hunters and fishermen who produced stone cookware and intricate basketry. Chumash society was hierarchical, with chieftains and shaman priests at the top of the pecking order and craftsmen and laborers at the bottom. Distinct Chumash dialects were spoken in each of dozens of villages.

The population began to diminish in the early 19th century with the establishment of five mission-based communities in Chumash territory, according to John R. Johnson, curator of anthropology at the Santa Barbara Museum of Natural History.

> **"** Some tribal leaders worry that the monthly casino check is simply a new form of dependency, as corrosive as the welfare payments of old. **"**

A 1798 survey counted about 1,200 Chumash in 14 villages in the Santa Ynez Valley. In 1804, Old Mission Santa Ines was built. By 1856, the number of Chumash in the valley had dropped to 109—a 90% decline caused largely by measles, smallpox and other diseases introduced from Europe.

A small cemetery next to the mission cathedral holds the remains of about 1,700 Indians, marked by crumbled tombstones and splintered crosses covered in moss. One small headstone reads simply: "Baby."

During the late 1800s, the Catholic Church relocated the Chumash in Santa Ynez to Zanja de Cota Ranch, a 99-acre flood plain. The church eventually donated the land to the Indians, and in 1906, the U.S. government created the nation's only federally recognized Chumash reservation.

This would become the tribe's salvation, giving the Santa Ynez band a sovereign territory on which to operate a casino. But at the time, there was no hint of such a windfall.

Life on the reservation was harsh. The Chumash lived in dilapidated adobe dwellings. Rosa Pace remembers the sight of families climbing into trees from rickety rooftops to escape the floodwaters of Zanja de Cota Creek. Alcohol abuse was rampant.

"Santa Ynez was a frontier town," says Johnson, who has studied the Chumash for three decades. "Some of the Indians developed into pretty rough customers. A couple of them ended up in San Quentin [State Prison]. But they persisted. They were people who made the best of what they had."

The Armenta clan embodies the tribe's impoverished past and its perseverance. Loreto and Florencia Armenta raised 10 children on the reservation during the Depression. The family lived in a lean-to without walls or windows and slept on steel cots lined up on a dirt floor. They bathed in a swimming hole and wore clothes made from discarded flour sacks.

"We didn't have anything," says Eva Pagaling, 80, one of the family's four surviving children.

Over the years, tribal members married into Mexican and Filipino families and grew detached from the reservation. Many left to work on the region's farms, picking fruits and vegetables.

In the early 1900s, the federal government began a decades-long practice of shipping Indian children to Catholic boarding schools.

"There was a movement to get Indian children away from their cultural awareness and teach them the West way," says Jim Fletcher, regional superintendent of the U.S. Bureau of Indian Affairs. "In the 1930s, the perspective was: 'How do we get them above the poverty line, get them an education and build them up.'"

Pagaling remembers the look of fear in her mother's eyes when federal agents showed up on the reservation. "Mother told us to go hide in the willows," she says. "She was afraid they would take us away."

Eventually, Pagaling and two sisters were sent to Saint Boniface School in Riverside County. Every morning at 6, the Native American boarding students were required to line up wearing oversized military boots, Pagaling recalled. Their chores included scrubbing toilets and mopping floors.

She and her sisters returned to the reservation after a year. Like many of their generation, they were unaware of their Chumash lineage.

"We thought we were poor Mexicans," she says.

Hitting the Jackpot

For many years, a rustic campground on the reservation provided the tribe's only source of steady revenue. The Chumash closed the site in the 1970s because it failed to generate enough money to cover the cost of utilities and water.

The band turned to gambling in 1983. A high-stakes bingo parlor attracted gamblers from as far as the San Francisco Bay Area and provided part-time employment for dozens of Indians.

"The days of begging for water are over," proclaimed then-tribal chairman Edward Olivas.

> *I'm not proud of getting money for doing nothing. . . . I want to do the best I can to earn it.*

But the bingo hall closed in 1988 because of rising debts and a business dispute with outside investors. It re-opened in 1990 in partnership with entertainer Wayne Newton, only to fold five months later, $250,000 in debt.

The band's run of bad luck ended in 1994. Following the lead of other Southern California tribes, the Chumash began offering slot-machine games, despite warnings from law enforcement authorities that the devices were illegal.

The casino's first general manager, Michael Lombardi, recalled gazing at a collapsed ceiling in the middle of the old bingo hall during his initial meeting with then-tribal chairman David Dominguez.

Outside, Chumash families huddled in the cold, waiting to receive surplus food from a tractor-trailer known as "the commodity truck."

"I want there to be a day when that truck no longer comes to my reservation." Lombardi recalled Dominguez telling him.

The band borrowed $600,000 to renovate the bingo facility and purchase 210 slot machines. Tribal members worked on the casino floor, provided security, directed parking and cooked burritos and fry bread for patrons.

Within three months, the band had paid off all of its start-up loans and installed 350 additional machines. The casino produced $31 million in revenue during its first year.

"When we put slot machines in that made $300 a day, everybody was in shock," Lombardi said.

Even more remarkable were the profit margins. By 2000, the tribe was collecting $70 million a year in revenue—and keeping 69% as profit, according to internal reports.

That same year, California tribes spent $24 million promoting a ballot initiative to legalize the reservation casinos and allow Indians to offer Las Vegas-style games of chance.

Proposition 1A passed, and casino revenue continued to soar. The Chumash spent $157 million on a new, Mediterranean-style gambling complex, which opened [in 2003]. The Chumash Casino Resort has 2,000 slot machines, a 106-room luxury hotel and an auditorium where Jay Leno, Fleetwood Mac and Whoopi Goldberg have performed.

The tribe recorded its first $1-million day in July [2004] and casino revenue is expected to surpass $200 million . . . a 40% increase from 2003.

Benefits to Tribe Members

The Chumash band allocates about 15% of its share of casino profits to the tribal government and various services and benefits. The remaining 85% is distributed directly to the 153 tribal members.

Only "enrolled members" of the Santa Ynez band—people who have one-quarter Chumash blood—are eligible for these monthly payments. Because Chumash frequently marry outside the tribe, most households have just one enrolled member.

Thousands of Chumash Indians outside Santa Ynez get no share of the riches because their separate tribes lack federal recognition. This is a source of bitter resentment in the broader Chumash nation.

"They've turned their backs on us," said Al-lu-koy Lotah, a Chumash medicine woman and leader of the 80-member Southern Owl clan.

The Santa Ynez tribal government has used gambling proceeds to repave roads, erect street lights and build a sewage treatment plant. It has also acquired adjacent property, expanding the reservation by 49 acres to accommodate future development. Within the next decade, Chumash leaders hope to build a school, a day care center, a health club and a bank.

They are also investing in higher education. Now, there are just four college graduates among the band's members. But in recent years, tribal subsidies have helped nearly 100 Chumash attend a university, community college or trade school.

[In 2003], the band achieved two "firsts" when one Chumash descendant enrolled in Stanford University and another graduated from law school—at the University of San Diego.

Like many Chumash elders, Eva Pagaling could never have

hoped to leave Santa Ynez for college. She worked for many years on an assembly line, packing frozen broccoli into food cartons.

> *Tribal subsidies have helped nearly 100 Chumash attend a university, community college or trade school.*

Pagaling still lives on the reservation, in the modest, stucco house she and her late husband bought in 1979. She still remembers the excitement of moving into the home, her first to have electrical outlets and natural gas.

As she ticked off the improvements in her life since the casino opened, Pagaling also spoke of the disorientation brought on by so much wealth.

She maintains her bearings, in part, by clinging to old habits. Pagaling still buys $6 shirts at thrift shops and discount stores. "I love Wal-Mart," she says. "I don't care if I have money or not. I want to be the way I always was."

Pagaling keeps putting off plans to buy a four-wheel drive sport utility vehicle to make the trip to her Lake Tahoe vacation home. She confesses to lingering regrets about the thousands of dollars she spent on a flat-screen television.

"I'm used to being poor and not having enough," she says. "I know I can afford things. But for me, to spend that money. . . . It's difficult."

Fast Spending

When gambling revenue began to flow in the mid-1990s, there was wide-spread fear that the casino would not last long; law enforcement officials had repeatedly threatened to shut it down.

"They spent the money as fast as they could," said Lombardi, the former casino manager. "They figured the gravy train was going to end."

Many members had never used banks and continued to store their money in tin cans and in glove compartments of abandoned vehicles. Today, most have bank accounts. But the impulse to spend quickly persists.

"A lot of these people lived a very primitive lifestyle," says financial advisor Stephen Drake, who has counseled tribal members on their finances. "They are going on a lot of trips and buying nice, very fancy cars. That, I believe, is human nature."

Tribal members privately acknowledge that some Chumash have gotten in over their heads, despite their robust casino income. In several cases, the band has garnished a member's share of gambling revenue to pay off debts.

Among those in financial distress is Gilbert Cash, the chairman of the tribal gaming commission who oversees gambling at the casino.

Cash, 38, has filed for personal bankruptcy twice in the past two years, piling up $128,502 in debts, including $60,000 in unpaid income taxes, according to court records. Cash says he fell behind because he wasn't prepared to be thrust into a higher tax bracket. Members who reside on the reservation pay only federal income taxes.

> *We're trying to tell kids there is more out there. Don't be content with just getting money.*

Battles over casino wealth have complicated marital breakups. [In 2002], the band decreed that tribal income, by "custom and tradition," is for the benefit of members only.

At the time, several Chumash members, including tribal chairman Vincent Armenta's sister, Maria Feeley, were embroiled in divorces.

Chumash attorneys have argued in court that Tribal Resolution 852 takes precedence over California's community property law. "We do not want the money to go to spousal support for nonmembers," attorney Lawrence Stidham said during a recent divorce proceeding.

Stidham said that all tribes "struggle . . . to protect and preserve" casino profits for Native Americans who have long endured unemployment and poverty.

In August [2004], a state appellate court ruled against the tribe in the Feeley case, clearing the way for her ex-husband, Randy Jacobsen, to collect $3,500 a month in alimony.

"When you think about it, it is astounding what the tribe is trying to get away with," said Vanessa Kirker, Jacobsen's attorney.

Other tribal members have succeeded in denying spouses a cut of gambling profits.

Lewis Gray said [he] has fought unsuccessfully for several years to compel his estranged wife, Cheryl, to make monthly support payments.

Gray, 45, who is not a member of the tribe, said Cheryl walked out on him several years ago, leaving him to provide for eight of their children, ages 6 to 17. He quit his job as a construction foreman, Gray said, to become a stay-at-home father in Fontana. He said he has run up $40,000 in credit card debt.

[In 2003], a judge ordered Cheryl to pay $12,166 a month in child support and alimony. Her family has made sporadic, partial payments. But the tribe has refused request from child-welfare officials to withhold the full amount from her casino checks, according to Gray and his attorney.

"My lawyer says we can't do anything about it because they are a sovereign nation," Gray says. "This is not fair to me and my kids. It's not right."

At a June divorce hearing involving Manuel Armenta, a brother of the tribal chairman, Stidham was asked how ex-spouses could support themselves if casino money was off-limits. The Chumash lawyer replied that they could throw themselves on the mercy of the tribe.

"I wouldn't put myself in the position of being humiliated," Armenta's wife, Zita, said in an interview. "That tribe would not do anything for me."

A Life of Comforts

Dominica Valencia raised her three children in a one-bedroom shack near the reservation. She ran her own doughnut shop in the mornings and worked as a housekeeper in the afternoons. For years, her husband, Michael, also held two jobs—as a welder and as a heavy equipment operator.

The Valencias no longer have to work. They donate their time to Native American programs, including the reservation clinic, pow-wows and a talking circle for Indian inmates at [nearby] Lompoc's federal penitentiary,

They also enjoy their newfound affluence. They own three homes and vacation in Hawaii every year. Once a week, they cook ribs on the backyard barbecue for their three dogs.

Yet along with the comforts have come unexpected complications.

The Valencias rarely entertain guests at home because the conversation often gets around to their casino riches. They were distressed several years ago to open their mailbox and find that the envelope containing the monthly check had been opened— apparently by someone unable to contain his curiosity.

"It always comes back to the money," Dominica says. "I get tired of that."

She and her husband worry about the effect of wealth on young people. The Valencias said they were floored one afternoon when their teenage son asked: "Where is my share?" They say they sat him down and explained that he is not entitled to an extravagant life-style just because he is Chumash.

Dominica, 44, a member of the tribe's education committee, is concerned that Chumash youths are growing accustomed to waiting for the casino check, just as their parents stood in line for surplus food.

"Some are going to college and building for the future," she says. "Then there are those who have no drive or ambition. . . . We're trying to tell kids there is more out there. Don't be content with just getting money."

6

Tribes Have Traded Sovereignty Rights for Casino Profits

Tim Giago

Tim Giago, an Oglala Lakota, is editor and publisher of the weekly Lakota Journal *in Rapid City, South Dakota. He is author of* The Aboriginal Sin *and* Notes from Indian Country.

While a few Indian tribes are making fortunes running casinos, these profits have come at a price. Most tribes have weakened their sovereignty rights, trading their independent nation status to state governments for permission to open gaming operations. In the bargain, the states have won the right to tax and regulate casinos on Indian land. As governments face massive budget deficits they are attempting to obtain more power on reservations, demanding casinos pay even higher taxes. Indian sovereignty is guaranteed in the U.S. Constitution, and tribal governments that have bargained it away to build casinos have committed a grave error that will not soon be rectified.

According to *U.S. News* [& *World Report*], 37 states [considered] gambling-related bills (in 2003). Politicians believe gambling is the easiest way to get money out of reluctant taxpayers.

Darrell West, director of the Taubman Center for Public Policy at Rhode Island's Brown University, said, "A lot of states have gotten addicted to gambling money, but it's a short-term fix that doesn't provide long-term stability."

South Dakota is one state facing a budget crisis. Gambling is legal in this state and mini-casinos can be found in nearly every community. Deadwood is a wide-open gaming town. Around $90 million was expected in revenues from the many casinos. Where has this windfall gone?

The state sets the agenda for the compacts signed with the nine Indian reservations in the state. But, the state collects no taxes from the few Indian casinos within its borders. Instead, the Indian tribes use the revenues in an effort to improve the living conditions on the reservations in a state where three reservation counties were counted among the top 10 poorest counties in America in the 2000 census.

South Dakota severely restricts the number of gaming devices and slot machines allowed in the casinos of the Indian nations. And this even though the tribes of this state were often the leaders in preserving their sovereign status from infringement by state government. I am often appalled at the freedoms given up by South Dakota tribes in order to open the door for the goose that lays the golden eggs: tribal casinos.

> *I am often appalled at the freedoms given up by South Dakota tribes in order to open the door for the goose that lays the golden eggs: tribal casinos.*

Acknowledging that gaming is raising the issues of tribal sovereignty, Anthony Pico, chairman of the Viejas Band of Kumeyaay Indians in San Diego County, said recently at a meeting of the National Indian Gaming Association, "Make no mistake, my friends, we are at war. Our sovereignty is under attack. But this is not a war of guns and bombs, it's a war of words. It's a war of perception and it's a war for truth."

Fine words, but about 16 years too late.

Gambling with Sovereign Status

When two of the most courageous tribal leaders in America said these very words in 1987, few tribal leaders were listening.

All most of them saw was that pot of gold at the end of their casino.

Wendell Chino served as chairman of the Mescalero Apache for more than 30 years. Roger Jourdain served as chairman of the Red Lake Band of Chippewa for more than 30 years. They took up the challenge to stand against the implementation of any gambling act that would infringe upon the sovereign rights of the Indian nations.

> *Indian nations sold out their sovereignty for the right to open casinos on their own land and gave up many freedoms in the process.*

They might as well have been whistling in the wind.

Any tribal leader who negotiated a compact with a state government was gambling with the sovereign status of his nation. Any capitulation made by that tribal leader was the same as opening the door to more infringement upon the sovereign status of his nation. This is a given.

State governments did not go quietly into the night when it came to preparing compacts for the Indian tribes within their borders. They held all of the cards and they knew how to play them.

When tribal governments such as the Mashentucket Pequots of Connecticut signed compacts that forced them to pay extortion money in the form of taxes to the state government, they opened up a can of worms that crawled across America.

Soon, states from New Mexico to Arizona were restructuring their compacts to include blood money from the tribes.

Chino and Jourdain have made the journey to the spirit world. But when they were alive, even up to the day they drew their last breaths, they condemned the Indian Gaming Regulatory Act as one that would bring an end to Indian sovereignty. They lashed out at those tribal leaders who signed gaming compacts with the state governments without considering the consequences.

Jourdain was still fighting for the sovereign rights of the Red Lake Band of Chippewa at his death. Chino was fighting the state of New Mexico to the wire about signing a gaming compact. He refused to surrender one ounce of sovereignty for a casino and, indeed, opened a casino without the blessing of a compact.

State government has seen what gaming can do for some lucky Indian tribes and they also see gaming as an easy way to cure their budget headaches.

Many Indian nations sold out their sovereignty for the right to open casinos on their own land and gave up many freedoms in the process. And now they are complaining that they are at war to protect their sovereign status. Horse hockey. All their leaders had to do was to read the writing in the gaming compacts they signed with the state governments to realize how much they were surrendering for that pot of gold.

State governments are now approaching the day of reckoning. The days of financial growth because of a strong economy are ending. They are looking at gambling as that "voluntary tax" to relieve their budget stress. The more they grow gambling, the more they infringe upon the solitary gaming status of the Indian nations. There are only so many gamblers to go around.

7

Tribes Abuse Their Sovereign Status to Avoid Government Regulation

Jan Golab

Jan Golab, a former editor with Los Angeles Magazine *and* Playboy, *is the author of* The Dark Side of the Force: A True Story of Corruption and Murder in the LAPD.

When the founding fathers included Indian sovereignty in the Constitution, they could not have envisioned tribes running multibillion-dollar gambling casinos near major population centers. Yet with the passage of the Indian Gaming Regulatory Act in 1989, tribes—and their white business backers—have been able to use sovereignty to gain an unfair advantage over their neighbors. While other citizens must pay sales and property taxes, and follow business regulations and zoning laws, sovereign tribes are not obligated to do so. While claiming to be independent entities, however, tribes remain dependent on state and federal government programs. Casinos create major problems for nearby residents, businesses, and police and fire departments while ignoring laws concerning traffic, public safety, the environment, and labor relations. It is unfair and undemocratic to give one group special privileges based on their ethnicity.

Foxwoods, the King Kong of casinos, was brought to Connecticut [by Pequot Indians] with dreams of untold riches. Now, locals are trying to kill the beast. Foxwoods and its sister institution, Mohegan Sun, (the world's two most profitable casinos), pay host state Connecticut a hefty $400 million a year—one fourth of the take. Yet in 2003, Connecticut became the first state in the country to pass legislation designed to halt any future casino development. The measure passed unanimously, not exactly a ringing endorsement for Indian gambling institutions. "Another gambling palace anywhere in the state would be disastrous," the *Hartford Courant* warned in an editorial. "The state must stop this slot-machine tsunami."

Jeff Benedict is president of the Connecticut Alliance Against Casino Expansion, and the author of *Without Reservation*, a book about the Mashantucket Pequot Indians and their Foxwoods casino. "Casino money costs us a lot more than it's worth," Benedict argues. He recites a litany of woes: Casinos have a negative impact on roads, water and land consumption, fire, police, ambulance service, air pollution, and traffic. Local school systems are flooded with the children of low-income casino workers, who also create a shortage of affordable housing. And there are social costs—increased bankruptcies, foreclosures, divorces, child abuse, and crime. "The closer a community gets to a casino, the higher those numbers are," says Benedict. "Who pays for that? The local and state governments."

> **"** *[The] Pequot tribe is illegitimate, a political contrivance based on sympathy and political correctness, not reality or common sense.* **"**

Casinos cause property devaluation and lost taxes when businesses and lands are taken over by tax-exempt tribes. While casino owners argue that they create jobs and help neighboring businesses, the casinos (which, as Indian enterprises, do not have to pay the same taxes or abide by the same laws as other establishments) actually damage competing businesses nearby—restaurants, bars, hotels, retail outlets. "When the Indian casino comes to town, nobody else does well," says Benedict.

Except for the lawyers. The Pequots have subjected their host state and local governments to a decade of legal battles over tribal land annexation, environmental and land-use regulations, and sovereign immunity from lawsuits and police jurisdiction. Local communities have spent millions litigating against further casino expansion. Twelve more would-be "tribes" are petitioning the Bureau of Indian Affairs for federal tribal status, and new land claims threaten over one-third of Connecticut's real estate.

> **//** *American Indians . . . are completely dependent on their host governments—for roads, power, water, fire and police protection, schools, universities, hospitals, and health care facilities.* **//**

Another book on Foxwoods, *Hitting the Jackpot*, by Wall Street reporter Brett Fromson, explains how a "tribe" that disappeared 300 years ago resurrected itself and won a gambling monopoly now worth $1.2 billion a year. Like Benedict, Fromson concludes that the re-created Pequot tribe is illegitimate, a political contrivance based on sympathy and political correctness, not reality or common sense—"the greatest legal scam."

Off the Tax Rolls

Next door in New York, the situation is even worse. The Empire State approved the Oneida Nation's Turning Stone Casino near Oneida ten years ago, without first obtaining any agreement for the Nation to share its revenues ($232 million in 2001) with the state, or any agreement to settle the tribe's claim to 250,000 acres of central New York land. Subsequent casino compacts with other tribes have been haphazard and subject to ongoing renegotiation, with New York collecting money from some, not from others.

The Oneidas have used their casino cash machine to buy 16,000 acres of land and businesses, including nearly all of the area's gasoline and convenience stores. Once they are Indian-owned, the land and businesses go off the tax rolls. The business impact and loss of property and sales taxes has some local communities teetering on bankruptcy. "The tribes hurt us in a number of ways," explains Scott Peterman, president of Upstate Citizens for Equality. "They buy a property and refuse to pay property tax because they say they are re-acquiring their ancient reservation. Then they open a business on that property and refuse to collect sales tax."

By undercutting all non-Indian businesses that collect taxes, tribal sales of gasoline and cigarettes alone cost New York state millions of dollars in annual taxes. The Supreme Court ruled in 1994 that states could tax tribal sales to non-native customers, but so far, New York has failed to enforce this over Indian resistance. One tribe, the Onondaga, sells an estimated 20,000 cartons of cigarettes every week, or $26 million worth a year. Governor George Pataki tried to collect in 1997, but he backed down when Indian protestors blocked the New York State Thruway. Last year [2003], the state legislature ordered Pataki to begin collecting the taxes, which it conservatively estimated would amount to $165 million in 2003 and $330 million in 2004. The *Syracuse Post-Standard* reported: "Indian Cig Sales Cost NY $435M." Another study estimated that New York tribes cost the state a total of $895 million last year. Still, the tab remains open.

> *Indian sovereignty . . . is a profoundly flawed special body of federal law—some say an outright scam—that creates bogus tribes, legalizes race-based monopolies, [and] creates a special class of super-citizens.*

The state with the most tribal casinos—82—is Oklahoma, where tribes rake in as much as $1.2 billion a year—and the state doesn't get a cent. Oklahoma Indians, who comprise 7 percent of the state population, have become the most powerful political force there. Meanwhile, officials estimate that Oklahoma's 39 tribes cost the state $500 million a year—in lost property taxes, lost revenues on tax-free cigarettes, and lost excise taxes and tag fees from cars sold by reservation dealerships. That's nearly the equivalent of the state's 2003 budgetary shortfall, enough to pay for 17,000 teachers. Meanwhile, the state's billion-dollar racetrack industry, which does pay taxes, is teetering on the edge of bankruptcy, and communities are mired in litigation with cash-flush tribes over land and water rights.

As Connecticut, New York, and Oklahoma wrestle to control their Indian casinos, California's casinos are rapidly expanding, and many other states, like Pennsylvania and Maryland, are just gearing up. Governor Arnold Schwarzenegger's [California] legacy will largely be a matter of whether or not he allows the Golden State to become the new Nevada. With their state monopoly on gambling, California Indians could eventually become the richest people on earth. Their 54 casinos are already raking in $5 billion a year, which isn't far behind the entire Las Vegas area ($7.7 billion), and they are pushing for more. With 107 federally recognized Indian reservations and rancherias—more than anywhere else in the country—California could easily surpass Nevada as the nation's gambling capital in the next few years.

Yet tribal chairmen blast the California governor for suggesting that they "pay their fair share." They insist that: "Governments cannot tax other governments!" They insist they are "sovereign."

"Sovereign" usually means "Independent." American Indians, however, are completely dependent on their host governments—for roads, power, water, fire and police protection, schools, universities, hospitals, and health care facilities. "The technical term for Indian reservations is 'domestic dependent nations,'" explains one legislative analyst. "They are not foreign governments. They have no foreign policy powers. They are not allowed to sell their land to anyone outside the U.S. and they are not allowed to maintain relations with any foreign nation. To regard them as being like foreign nations inside our nation is very problematic. How can Congress create a government within a state, with powers that Congress itself could never possess?"

The notion that American Indian tribes should be treated like Canada or France, as some tribal leaders assert, offends common sense. "A nation within the nation" is what they claim to be, but it is not even close to a reality. If they are independent nations, why have Indians been allowed to donate over $150 million to U.S. political campaigns and become our nation's most influential political special interest group? . . .

"Mend It or End It"

"The debate over Indian sovereignty may seem abstract," explains one analyst, "but it gets very concrete when a state suddenly loses authority over a major portion of its land. Reservation shopping basically gives wealthy gambling tribes the ability to shrink counties and states"—and to place important personal actions and economic transactions beyond the reach of American law. Throughout the nation, whenever U.S. citizens battle tribes over problems with land, water, zoning disputes, personal injuries, firings, broken contracts, or other issues, the claim of tribal sovereignty often intervenes. As tribal governments expand, local governments lose their political power to protect their citizens, some of whom find themselves ruined by tribal sovereignty claims—like the rancher who lost all his water to a new tribal golf course and resort.

The Citizens Equal Rights Alliance and United Property Owners, umbrella organizations encompassing hundreds of grassroots groups affected by Indian sovereignty claims, represent some 3.5 million citizens and business and property owners affected by America's 550-plus Indian reservations. There are also independent organizations in 22 states, like One Nation in Oklahoma, Upstate Citizens for Equality in New York, and Stand Up for California.

> *Indian tribes now spend more on elections than any other interest group in America.*

Activists in this rapidly growing anti-sovereignty movement feel betrayed by their elected leaders. Indian sovereignty, they say, is a profoundly flawed special body of federal law—some say an outright scam—that creates bogus tribes, legalizes race-based monopolies, creates a special class of super-citizens immune to the laws that govern others, and Balkanizes America. "Sovereign rights based on race for a few American citizens is not, and will never be, reconcilable with the equality and civil rights guaranteed by the United States Constitution to all citizens," says Scott Peterman, of Upstate Citizens for Equality. "The concepts of equal rights, equal opportunities, equality under the law, and equal responsibilities for all citizens should not be bargained away by our politicians."

Many say that sovereignty is a concept from another age that no longer works today. "It goes back a century to when native populations had been dispossessed," explains former California senator Pete Wilson, "to when the U.S. was largely an agricultural nation and we did not have the kind of economy we have today." Wilson says that when the Indian Gaming Regulatory Act (IGRA) was enacted in 1988, it didn't get nearly the attention it deserved. "A lot of people [in Congress] voted for it thinking that it amounted to little more than Bingo on reservations. . . . They didn't see it as a commercial enterprise that would transform reservations and their surrounding communities."

> *// The states now facing the biggest budget deficits are also the states with the largest number of tax-exempt Indian casinos and tax-evading tribal businesses. //*

Most analysts concur that IGRA is a terrible law—vague fuzzy, and unclear. "Congress should have spelled out much more clearly what the tribes are allowed to do," explains one analyst. "IGRA has subsequently been interpreted by the courts to mean that a state can pass a ballot initiative granting a lucrative monopoly on gambling, based solely on race, within a state that does not otherwise allow gambling. It defies the basic principles of equal protection, and gives cause to wonder. Should we give Hispanics the liquor industry? Should blacks get cigarettes? What about the Asian boat people?". . .

Experts contend that Congress never intended sovereign status for every parcel of land granted to Indians. The small California [reservations called] rancherias, for example, were meant to host housing projects for landless Indians. One such group of federal housing recipients-turned-Indian-tribe, the Auburns, have used their new sovereign status to open the massive Thunder Valley casino near Sacramento. The Auburns are descendants of 40 Indians who were set up on a few dozen acres of public housing in 1910. "Do you really think Congress intended for them to be a sovereign nation over which state law would have no force?" asks one legislative analyst who specializes in Indian law.

When it comes to sovereignty, everyone seems to agree that Congress will eventually have to "mend it or end it." Congress has the power to shape and re-shape the relevant laws as it sees fit. The problem is a lack of will, due largely to ignorance or fear of the fast-growing political clout of tiny gambling-enriched tribes who have shown a great willingness to use their lucre for political donations. . . .

And while many in Congress are having second thoughts about tribal sovereignty, others continue to work to expand it, sometimes with the enticement of ample campaign donations. Senator Elizabeth Dole has a bill calling for recognition of the Lumbee Nation of North Carolina, and fellow Republican, Senator George Allen, is backing a measure to recognize six new tribes in Virginia. The Native Hawaiian Bill would grant tribal status to some 400,000 Hawaiians, creating the biggest tribe in the country and virtual apartheld in the fiftieth state. "Tribal sovereignty is going to be a hard thing to beat because the politicians are ignorant," says Scott Peterman. "They think sovereignty is good for the Indians, but it isn't. It's good for the tribal governments, not for individual Indians.". . .

A Racially Charged Issue

Despite Arnold Schwarzenegger's success in standing up to the Indian tribes of California, most elected officials are afraid to address the issue of sovereignty. Like Social Security and illegal immigration, some view it as a "third rail" issue—touch it and you die. Some Indians insist that sovereignty is the essence of being an American Indian, so they respond to any questioning of sovereignty as a personal attack on Indians. Those who question sovereignty are frequently denounced as racist. Former Washington senator Slade Gorton was actually a defender of tribal sovereignty except when it trampled on non-Indian rights, and for even that mild reservation, he was branded "The Indian Fighter" and demagogued as racist, which contributed to his narrow defeat in 2000 by Maria Cantwell.

Because of the volatility of the sovereignty issue, more than a dozen senators and congressmen declined to be interviewed for this story. Many of their aides who did talk asked not to be identified. "Politicians are afraid to speak out and have their views seen in print," explains one activist, "because then tribes will spend big money to get them un-elected." Indeed, Indian tribes now spend more on elections than any other interest group in America.

"Tribal gaming has created a terrific inequality between tribes, and the people who have benefited are only a tiny percentage of American Indians," says one government official who asked not to be identified. "If you're a bogus six-member tribe with a fabulous location for a casino, all six of you get tremendously wealthy. But if you're a genuine, historic tribe in a remote location, like the Standing Rock Sioux of North Dakota, you accrue little or no benefit." Indeed, almost half of the nation's Indian population lives in five states—Montana, Nevada, North Dakota, South Dakota, and Oklahoma—that account for only a small percentage of Indian gaming revenues.

The same official is skeptical that any politician will have the guts to stand up to the Indians until everyday Americans are up in arms. He even bets that Governor Schwarzenegger will go belly-up on the issue. "I've seen too many elected officials challenge the tribes, then gradually work their way back to an accommodation. At the end of the day, he'll be a blood brother.". . .

Practice Sovereignty Responsibility

Many experts believe it will take years before the inevitable day of reckoning on sovereignty finally reaches the halls of Congress. But the public mood is changing rapidly in certain places. Some observers believe this subject could mature into a bona fide political issue much sooner.

As executive director of United Property Owners and a national spokesperson for One Nation, Barb Lindsay represents more than 300,000 property owners, scores of grassroots community groups, dozens of local governments, and thousands of small businesses. Part Indian herself, Lindsay has been lobbying in Washington for ten years. She has emerged as one of the leading voices in the growing national movement challenging tribal sovereignty.

"Five years ago, people didn't know anything about tribal sovereignty," Lindsay explains. "Indian gaming has really elevated the issue in terms of public awareness, and with elected officials and their staffs. A few years ago they were not very sympathetic to our cause, because all they knew was tribal positions. But with growing problems in states like Connecticut, California, Wisconsin, New York, Oregon, Washington, and Oklahoma, more Congressmen are having problems in their own districts. They see tribes running roughshod over local citizens, ignoring environment laws and land-use codes and water rights. Instead of the *Dances with Wolves* Hollywood mythology they've been sold, they are now facing the reality of dealing with a group of people who believe they are somehow above the law."

The true meaning of sovereignty, Lindsay says, is tax evasion. "It is no coincidence that the states now facing the biggest budget deficits are also the states with the largest number of tax-exempt Indian casinos and tax-evading tribal businesses. It is widely recognized that IGRA is being abused and Indian casino reservation shopping is undermining local, county, and state tax bases and changing community character and quality of life, while simultaneously denying local citizens a voice in how the future of their community will be shaped."

Others concur that America's tribes need to practice sovereignty in a way that is responsibly congruent with the laws of their "host nations" (state and local governments). If Indians choose the endless warpath, some observers say, they will eventually lose the war, and "sovereignty." This is difficult for some tribes to accept, because they have achieved their current success and financial bonanzas through two decades of aggressive court battles and relentless warfare with the states. But that war is over and they have won. They now need a new, cooperative strategy, or they may awaken resistance in their neighbors.

Many groups have been mistreated in history—blacks, Jews, Asians, Poles, the Irish. "Should each of these groups be given a sovereign land within the United States and allowed to govern as they choose, free from taxes that must be paid by others, and free to engage in activities denied to others?" asks Henry Lamb, chairman of Sovereignty International. "Americans are defined not by color, religion, or ethnicity, but by a belief in, and dedication to, the principle of freedom, as defined in our founding documents. As a nation, we seem to have forgotten this fundamental principle."

8

Indian Casinos Have No Obligation to Share Profits with the Government

Steve Newcomb

Steve Newcomb is the Indigenous Law Research Coordinator at Kumeyaay Community College, a school on the Sycuan Indian Reservation near San Diego, California.

In recent years, many states have experienced huge financial shortfalls, forcing cutbacks in many areas of government. Politicians who have mismanaged budgets are now expecting Indian tribes to bail them out by sharing profits from successful casinos. In California the governor has made emotional appeals to constituents, demanding that tribes pay their "fair share." To Native Americans and their supporters this seems like a cruel joke. Tribes have been paying since the first Europeans set foot in America. They have been repeatedly stripped of their culture, their land, and their very existence by demagogues who wanted land, forests, and other natural resources. Today the government wants profits from casinos. Tribes are sovereign nations that owe nothing to Americans. In fact, citizens of the United States have an immeasurable debt to Native Americans who suffered so that others could prosper.

I ndian land is one key factor that has fueled the economy of the United States for the more than two hundred years since the end of the Revolutionary War. The revolutionaries who founded the United States saw the sale of Indian lands as the primary means of paying off the huge debt that the Confederacy had accumulated during the war for independence. Indeed, to the extent that the United States has been considered a political experiment, it has been an experiment predicated upon the dispossession of Native nations and the violent appropriation of their lands. The American motto "life, liberty, and the pursuit of happiness" could have been more correctly written, "life, liberty, and the pursuit of Indian land."

From a cynical point of view, we might say that U.S. policy makers considered it appropriate to dispossess the Indian nations and take their lands in order to make those indigenous nations "pay their fair share" to the "progress" and expansion of the American empire. The Indians had millions of acres of land that the United States wanted, and, from the white peoples' point of view, the Indians ought to be paying their "fair share" of lands and resources to the future development of the United States, regardless of the fact this would necessarily involve the destruction of their traditional Native economy and way of life.

> **It is highly ironic for Native peoples to be accused of not being 'fair' to a state historically responsible for destructive, even genocidal policies against them.**

During his successful 2003 campaign for Governor of California, then gubernatorial candidate Arnold Schwarzenegger followed this long tradition of expecting Indian nations to fuel the economy of the dominant society. He did so by putting a tremendous amount of money into television ads claiming that Indian "gaming tribes" are not paying their "fair share" of gaming revenues to the State of California, a state now wracked by record deficits. Apparently, Schwarzenegger saw the revenues realized by Indian nations and peoples in California as promising to offset a major part of California's current fiscal crisis.

To put it mildly, it is highly ironic for Native peoples to be accused of not being "fair" to a state historically responsible for destructive, even genocidal policies against them. This article will attempt to put Mr. Schwarzenegger's charge against the Indian peoples of California into the historical context of the horrendously damaging policies that the Native peoples of California have been subjected to over the generations.

> *Miraculously, the Native peoples of California have survived several waves of colonization, and are now thriving to an extent not possible even twenty years ago.*

One meaning of the word "fair" is "free from bias, dishonesty, or injustice," such as "a fair decision" or "a fair judge." A "share" is "the full or proper portion or part allotted, belonging to, contributed by, or owed by an individual or group." Key terms here are "belonging to" and "owed by an individual or group." This article argues that to claim Indian gaming revenues actually "belong" to California, or that a portion of those monies are "owed" by Native peoples to California, is to defy logic, history, and historical accountability, not to mention the political identity of sovereign Indian nations and peoples.

Given that roughly 73,340,000 acres of ancestral lands and ecosystems have been historically torn away from the Native peoples of California; given the history of abuse, genocide, enslavement, and injustice that Native peoples experienced during the colonization of California; and given the way Native peoples were stripped of their free and independent way of life, along with a vast amount of the thousands of years of accumulated cultural wisdom and understanding, I find it inconceivable that Native peoples "owe" anything to the state of California, or that any portion of Indian gaming revenues rightfully "belongs" to the state.

The Historical Context

California is a geographic area encompassing some 75 million acres, or 155,650 square miles. Today, according to the Sacramento office of the Bureau of Indian Affairs, the amount of Indian land in California is some 660,000 acres. This means that Indian peoples have been deprived of some 74,340,000 acres of land in California, lands and ecosystems which include coastlines and beaches, deserts, mountains, rivers and other waterways such as springs and aquifers, as well as forests and scenic places of breathtaking beauty such as Yosemite, the giant Sequoias, and the Redwoods. Prior to the European invasion, virtually all the lands and natural resources that now serve as the foundation of the world's sixth largest economy were in the possession of and utilized by the Native peoples of California.

For thousands and thousands of years prior to European arrival to the Americas, indigenous peoples had been living free and independent in the region of North America now called California. Over millennia, the Native peoples evolved and accumulated a degree of knowledge and wisdom that enabled them to maintain a viable existence even in difficult climates that experienced periodic droughts that would sometimes last for more than a decade. Over the course of eons, the Native peoples of California clearly demonstrated a genius for adaptation to the different climes, terrains, and ecosystems found in their region of the planet.

> *Each distinct Native nation, people, tribe, or [reservation], is a sovereign body politic that predates and is politically separate from the State of California.*

There are also many other discrete time frames to consider since the advent of colonization. [More than] 460 years have passed since October 7, 1542, when the Portuguese explorer Juan Rodriguez Cabrillo made landfall at Point Loma at the San Diego harbor. This is a period of more than four and a half centuries marked by Native resistance to disease, Catholic "missions", massacres, enslavement, unratified treaties, forced assimilation, and acculturation. As a direct result, the population of Native peoples declined precipitously during this period.

To give the reader some sense of the magnitude of population decline, one estimate places the Native population in California at over 300,000 in 1769. By 1900 the combined population of Native people in California is estimated to have amounted to roughly 17,000, with 100,000 (if not more) having perished in the twenty-year period between 1848 and 1868.

This precipitous drop of the Native population from 300,000 to 17,000 is an overall loss of some 283,000 people in one hundred thirty one years, or the loss of roughly 94% of the original 300,000 in thirteen decades. But if we were to take the initial estimate of 300,000 Native people, and postulate an ordinary birth rate, think of what the Native population would have been under ordinary conditions and circumstances absent this massive death rate. . . .

Much Has Been Lost

Any historical account of the Indians of California will necessarily be only a partial picture of what took place in the past. There is so much we cannot possibly know because of the amount of firsthand information lost in the past as Indian people died of diseases or massacres, without any means of recording their knowledge for posterity. Anyone inclined to doubt this statement has only to think of the vast amount of Native oral history that was carried to the grave and never recorded in a written form. Although there are many Native people alive today who carry some degree of oral history, none are likely to deny that much has been lost. What is most readily available to us now is the written record of the past, which, until fairly recently, was generally filtered through the non-Indian consciousness and cultural biases.

One conclusion we can state unequivocally, however, is that Native peoples existed in the geographical region now called California for many thousands of years prior to the appearance of Christian Europeans [in] the region. They continue to exist. Having said this, it is also beyond dispute that non-Indian colonization of the region has had an incredibly destructive effect on every conceivable aspect of the way of life of the Native peoples.

The colonizing peoples of Western Christendom (as Europe was referred to when Cabrillo, sailing under the Spanish flag, first made landfall in what is now called San Diego harbor) believed themselves to possess a divine right to take over and rule the lands of the entire hemisphere and to transform, remake, or destroy the Native peoples. Miraculously, the Native peoples of California have survived several waves of colonization, and are now thriving to an extent not possible even twenty years ago. Native communities, while still beset with their share of the problems every human community deals with, are nonetheless experiencing a resurgence of languages, songs, basketry, and spiritual traditions. Economically, many Native peoples are thriving as a result of casino revenues. However, it is also important to keep in mind that not all Native communities in California have gaming institutions. Many are still having a hard time economically, having been historically beaten down and deprived of a viable economic base in their own ancestral lands.

In any event, the idea that the Indians of California "owe" the State of California a portion of their gaming revenues is preposterous, particularly in light of what the Native peoples of California have been subjected to by the dominant society. Each distinct Native nation, people, tribe, or rancheria [California reservation], is a sovereign body politic that predates and is politically separate from the State of California. The Indigenous peoples of California do not, therefore, "owe" the State of California any of [their] gaming proceeds, any more than Mexico "owes" a portion of its lottery proceeds to the United States. Phrased differently, no part of Indian gaming proceeds rightfully "belong" as a "fair share" to the State of California.

Nonetheless, political agreements known as "gaming compacts" have been and will continue to be worked out between Native nations and the State of California, pursuant to the Indian Gaming Regulatory Act. What we ought to never lose sight of, however, is the fact that the broader context for such political agreements is the historical oppression and dispossession that Native nations have been subjected to in their own backyard.

9

Gaming Tribes and States Need to Work Together to Help All Citizens

Susan Masten

Susan Masten is the former president of the National Congress of American Indians (NCAI), the oldest and largest tribal government organization in the United States. NCAI works with its membership of more than 250 tribal governments to formulate policy concerning sovereignty, gaming issues, law enforcement, environmental protection, and other issues.

The issue of Indian sovereignty has created conflicts between gaming tribes and state governments. This is unfortunate because tribes and states have many shared interests, and the growth of the casino industry has been beneficial to both Indians and non-Indians. When tribes can use casino profits to build schools, roads, clinics, and other community facilities, states have less pressure to provide for tribe members. States and tribes need to cooperate to resolve their disagreements and find solutions that benefit both parties.

Editor's note: The following selection is from a speech by Susan Masten, representing the National Congress of American Indians, delivered to the National Governor's Association.

I would like to begin by discussing the broader context within which these specific issues [between tribes and states] arise. Here at the national level, too often we act as if the relationships between states and tribes are little more than jurisdictional battles over the hot button issues, and we ignore the many similarities between states and tribes that offer great opportunities for cooperation.

> *Tribes and states have a great deal in common because we share one very unique and fundamental attribute: we are both sovereign governments.*

At the local level, states and tribes have lots of mutual interests: law enforcement, health care, family services, natural resources, to name just a few. Our front line workers and your front line workers are working together every day. Tribes and states also have a lot in common in other ways. Both tribal governments and state governments are confronted by limited budgets that we have to use efficiently, while trying to provide comprehensive services to our citizens. We're trying to promote economic development while at the same time protect the environment and our quality of life. In short, tribes and states have a great deal in common because we share one very unique and fundamental attribute: we are both sovereign governments.

Tribal Self-Determination

The fact that states and tribes are both sovereign governments should be better understood than it is. Everyone knows that the U.S. Constitution set up our federal system of government, but how many people know that the Constitution also recognizes the sovereignty of Indian tribes? Far too few. Hundreds of treaties, Supreme Court decisions, federal laws and executive orders have repeatedly affirmed that Indian Nations retain our fundamental and inherent powers of self-government. Most people are not aware of this because it is not taught in our schools.

Why is there so little understanding of tribal government in our country? The reason is found in our history. Indian tribes have been forcibly moved from one end of the country to another, our lands and resources have been stolen despite the guarantees of treaties and federal laws, and finally, when there was little left to take from us, our rights and needs have simply been ignored. This is the dark history we have inherited. A history which all of us need to understand better.

Indian tribes have not disappeared as so many thought we would. Despite enormous poverty, suffering and pressures to assimilate, Indian people have stayed together and continued to raise our children and teach them our traditions and languages, and have struggled to maintain our sovereignty and our lands. Tribes have struggled and succeeded in establishing the federal policy of tribal self-determination that was created in 1970 by President Nixon and has been endorsed by every succeeding U.S. President including our President [in 2001], President George W. Bush. Since that time, tribes are growing stronger than ever, people are moving home to the reservations, economic development is beginning to take hold in many places, and our government structures are growing ever more effective and secure.

> *Gaming in some parts of Indian Country has created jobs, provided economic growth and allowed investment in education, health care and housing, among other programs.*

Why have we done this? Why did our parents and grandparents and all of the great tribal leaders work so hard to reestablish tribal sovereignty? It is not because of some abstract principle or because of a sense of entitlement. It is because tribal self-government is critical for us to maintain our cultures and our viability as distinct groups of people. It is because we want our children to grow up with the same traditions and values that we grew up with. These are reasons that everyone in America can understand because these are the basic values of cultural survival that we all share just as much as our need to breathe the air.

Although there are these common threads that run through all of tribal history, it is really unfair to generalize because Indian tribes all over the country are so distinct and our histories and circumstances vary so widely. This is a point that I would like to emphasize: it is very difficult to generalize about tribes. Just as California is not like Rhode Island, Indian tribes have a great deal of diversity in size, culture, land base, values and economic systems. Just as states need different laws and policies, so do tribes need different laws and policies to fit with their unique circumstances.

Economic Opportunities

Tribes and states also share social and economic systems and we are experiencing changes that can affect our relationship. A good example of this is the growing suburbs and exurbs throughout the West. The 2000 census shows that the U.S. population is dramatically expanding into areas that were once very rural. Well, these same areas are where our reservations are. So on one hand it is no wonder that we are experiencing some growing pains as Americans move into Indian Country. The conflicts didn't occur as often when population densities were extremely low.

> *Indian gaming results in the reduction in welfare payments and unemployment rates for Indian and non-Indian communities.*

On the other hand, the population growth has brought economic opportunities to a number of Indian reservations where they simply did not exist before. This is good news for both tribes and states. If there is one thing we agree on, it is that we need to promote jobs for our citizens. As responsible governments we need to sit down at the table and work for mutually acceptable solutions to the growing pains—with the knowledge that these issues too will be resolved.

The transformations in the tribal economy are causing alarm in some places. Particularly with tribal gaming, tribes have been repeatedly challenged on their ability to raise revenue and create jobs. But tribal governmental gaming has grown at about the same rate as state gaming. Thirty-seven states and the District of Columbia now have state lotteries. Much of this growth in state-sponsored gaming was a direct result of budget deficits in the 1980's. States found state lotteries to be a good solution because it allowed them to raise revenue without raising taxes. State lotteries invest in education, the environment and other important programs. Tribal governments have pursued governmental gaming for similar reasons. That is, before gaming, many Indian nations were unable to fund basic government services for their people. Gaming in some parts of Indian Country has created jobs, provided economic growth and allowed investment in education, health care and housing, among other programs.

Moreover, tribal gaming has brought substantial beneficial economic and social impacts to surrounding communities. In fact, there is national evidence that Indian gaming results in the reduction in welfare payments and unemployment rates for Indian and non-Indian communities. I know that we will continue to argue over Indian gaming, but sometimes I can't figure out why we are having this argument in the first place. . . .

I think it is important to understand the social and historic context of these issues so that we can understand the role that both states and tribes have played in creating the issue, and then we sit at the table, government-to-government, and work out agreements that will be mutually acceptable. I don't believe that we want to hand this issue over to the federal government to resolve. We know that we will arrive at agreements that are much closer to what we want as state leaders and as tribal leaders by working together.

10

Indian Casinos Lead to Gambling Addiction

Candi Cushman

Candi Cushman is an associate editor for Citizen Magazine, *a publication of Focus on the Family, an organization
whose mission is to disseminate the Christian gospel and to
preserve traditional values and the institution of family.*

As the number of Indian casinos has increased, so has
the number of gambling addicts. While pro-gaming factions promote casinos as a risk-free way to improve life
on Indian reservations, some Native Americans have
become victims in their own casinos, gambling away
their paychecks every week. Reservation gambling addiction leads to increased family strife, divorce, alcoholism, and even suicide. For these reasons, a majority
of Navajos have rejected overtures from the Indian-
gaming industry to build casinos. However, while there
are no casinos on the reservation of America's largest
tribe, others have been built nearby. These border casinos have created problems for some Navajos who have
become addicted to gambling.

Some call it America's Third World, this forgotten land of
strange, mythic rock formations that jut dramatically from
the ground, where towering red cliffs are interspersed with dilapidated wooden shacks, occasional tepees and lonely trailers.
It seems such a strange contrast—this abject poverty in the
midst of majestic creation, with its telltale signs of a culture in
decline: bright yellow "don't drink, don't drive" signs and tiny

white crosses marking drunken-driving accidents dotting the highway every few miles.

Welcome to the Navajo Nation, an enchanting yet tragic land, whose 298,000 tribe members—more than half spread over a 17-million-acre land mass roughly the size of West Virginia—have struggled for centuries to overcome poverty, addiction and fragmented families. But now some people say they have found the Navajos' salvation: casinos.

> **"**Housewives, tribal leaders and former medicine men . . . believe gambling will destroy, not save, their people.**"**

"More senior citizens get quality health care, more children can afford a college education . . . and every Indian tribe has equal opportunity," promised pro-gambling commercials that accosted Arizona television viewers this spring [2002]. Against a backdrop of sunny-faced Native American children, plaintive elderly men and young families, the ad urged voters to support efforts to expand gambling over the next two decades because "our future demands nothing less."

Similar emotional, quick-money pitches intended to guilt-trip communities into approving Indian casinos have successfully spread through Louisiana, California and New York in recent years. But those behind this latest advertising blitz have neglected to mention an important fact: The majority of voters in the Navajo Nation—America's largest Indian tribe, covering New Mexico, Arizona and Utah—oppose gambling. So much so, they voted it down twice. [Arizona tribes such as the Yavapai have been running casinos since 1990.]

During a trip across the Southwest, *Citizen* met these voters —an array of Native Americans that includes housewives, tribal leaders and former medicine men—who believe gambling will destroy, not save, their people.

Beware "The Gambler"

It's 10 A.M. on Friday, and 88 Navajo Council delegates have assembled at the tribe's Capitol in Window Rock, Ariz.—named for a huge sandstone rock that, like a giant peephole into the sky, is punctured with a perfectly eroded circle. Beside the rock sits the Navajo Council Chamber, a round stone fort.

Inside, Delegate Edison Wauneka, chairman of the Navajo Public Safety Committee, complains that casino ads give Native Americans a one-sided view of gambling: "What we don't get is the other side, the dark side—what's happening to the families, people addicted to it, the children. The government is not making that known to the people; they are trying to cover that up."

While gambling advocates promise new jobs and better health care at the expense of rich white tourists, Wauneka sees a different reality. He sees it in the lines of elderly Navajos with Social Security checks in their pockets and single moms hoping for extra rent money who greet off-reservation casino buses at dawn. He sees it in the faces of Indian children confiscated by social services whose mothers left them to play the slots. And he sees it in the fathers addicted to gambling who have started trickling into the tribe's addiction-recovery offices.

> *The first monster ... alcoholism has swept our people. Now there is a second monster our government is trying to release—gambling.*

Add to that the scourge of alcoholism—as evidenced by the victims of alcohol-related accidents featured weekly in the *Navajo Times'* obituary section. According to a study released [in] December [2001] by New York's State University at Buffalo Research Institute on Addictions, problem drinkers are 23 times more likely to have a gambling problem. The study also found that pathological gambling is "significantly higher among minorities and lower-income individuals," which doesn't bode well for Navajos, since at least 50 percent of them depend on welfare.

What American people don't understand, explains Milton Shirleson—a one-time Navajo medicine man turned Christian pastor—is the devastation wrought by introducing gambling into a society already crippled by alcoholism and poverty. Decades of welfare dependency and addiction have steadily ravaged his people, and now Shirleson fears gambling will strike the final blow.

"A lot of our Navajo people go to the [Arizona] border casinos, and they mix that with alcohol," Shirleson says. "The husband gambles his money away, comes home, the money is tight, there's an argument and the guy goes drinking and domestic violence increases. . . . It's increasing because gambling is so accessible."

Standing beside a wooden church sign depicting an open Bible and the verse "The truth will set you free," Shirleson says he has counseled roughly 150 Indian families hurt by gambling addictions: "The first monster I call alcoholism has swept our people. Now there is a second monster our government is trying to release—gambling."

Long before the advent of casinos, he says, ancient Navajo folklore warned of this new monster. Elderly Navajos still tell stories about a mysterious character called The Gambler who tricked Navajo people out of everything they owned and made them slaves until the people overcame him and shot him to heaven on a rocket. To this day, the story goes, The Gambler bides his time in heaven, waiting for an opportune moment to exact revenge.

Though their tribe has traditionally outlawed on-site gambling, it seems the specter has indeed returned to haunt the Navajos—in the form of U.S. governors offering tempting bargains and peer pressure created by other tribes joining the bandwagon.

This spring [2001] Arizona Gov. Jane Dee Hull pushed for legislative approval of a compact allowing unprecedented gambling expansion in exchange for more state regulation and an estimated $83 million state share in casino profits—despite a federal judge's ruling that governors don't have the power to bind the state in tribal gambling deals. After their proposal failed, Hull and leaders from 17 tribes joined forces to get the compact on the November ballot.

> *They said they would train people . . . but when a nontribal person comes in with skills and money, he gets the top position.*

Feeling the pressure, Navajo leaders signed an ordinance [in] October [2002] allowing individual tribe chapters (political entities similar to states) to seek exemption from tribal gambling prohibitions—even though thousands of Navajos like Shirleson voted down casinos during reservation-wide referendums in 1994 and 1997. So far, leaders of at least three chapters have requested exemptions, spurring fears that gambling will spread across the reservation.

"It's already been a problem with all the casinos surrounding the area," says 57-year-old Jerry Gohns, a member of To'hajiilee, the first Navajo chapter allowed an exemption. Of the eight employees Gohns oversees as transportation director at the chapter high school, "seven are going [gambling]," he says. "When they get paid, the following week they ask to borrow money—even just three dollars. That's how bad it is."

Empty Promises

A few miles away, one of the nation's oldest Indian pueblos, Laguna, offers ominous foreshadowing of where the Navajos could be headed. Like the Navajo Nation, Laguna once forbade gambling and alcohol; but now the pueblo, a rustic collection of adobe homes and ranches near Albuquerque, N.M., has two new casinos and a grocery aisle full of beer and wine.

"We stood against gambling for the longest time," says Richard Delores, a Laguna native whose grandfather was a tribal high priest. "I can remember saying, 'This tribe will never give in to gaming; this tribe will stand.'

"But little by little, some of the old folks died out and some younger ones came into political positions, and the foundation crumbled."

An obnoxious gold-shaped dome that seems an affront to the serene red cliffs behind it, the Laguna-owned Dancing Eagle Casino uses a gleaming white Nissan draped with a "Win Me" banner to attract customers. You can only win the car by betting, Delores says, as he waves to a cousin driving a casino bus and then greets a man gambling inside who works for the tribe's housing department. The man is surrounded by other Native Americans sitting in a dark, smoke-filled room, spellbound by multi-colored slot machines. The only visible Caucasians are two truck drivers and a retired couple.

Just down the road is the pueblo's other casino, The Laguna Travel Center, where fields of red dirt are being cleared for 1,000 slot machines, a golf course and RV parking lots. Despite the construction, a hastily erected box-like structure tempts locals with 95 slot machines. Inside, an elderly Navajo couple with sunken eyes and withered faces confess they come here often because "our nation doesn't allow it."

"We never win," admits the wife, with quiet resignation. But before she can reveal how much they've lost that day, a security guard escorts *Citizen* outside for asking too many questions.

Yet statistics reveal what casinos work so hard to hide. Like the fact that most nonmetropolitan gambling operations draw most of their customers from a 35- to 55-mile radius, according to the U.S. Gambling Study conducted by the University of Massachusetts at Amherst. "When you have that kind of impact, you are not bringing in new dollars. You are drawing out money from local enterprises," says the study's director, Robert Goodman.

And even though casinos lure locals, the profits have yet to translate into big bucks for Laguna tribe members, says Delores, who was offered a job at the casino for $6 an hour—half of what he makes as a pesticide man. Meanwhile, some of the community benefits promised by gambling promoters—like more prison space—have yet to materialize two years into the casino's operation.

Delores, who gets inside access to spray both casinos, is also bothered by the fact that he never sees Indian managers. "They said they would train people . . . but when a nontribal person comes in with skills and money, he gets the top position."

> *// When you consider that unemployment is anywhere from 46 to 50 percent, to create 3,000 jobs from gambling would only reduce that rate by 1 percent. //*

His observations are on target: The National Indian Gaming Association told *Citizen* that of the 300,000 jobs provided by 321 Indian gambling operations nationwide, 75 percent are held by non-Indians. And though Indian gambling has sky rocketed since 1990, "the vast majority of American Indians . . . have not realized the early 'high hopes' of the casino boom," according to an Associated Press computer analysis of unemployment, poverty and public-assistance records released in September 2000.

One of the only studies of its kind, the analysis found that unemployment on reservations stayed at about 54 percent between 1991 and 1997 despite the casino boom. "Overall, the new [casino] jobs have not reduced unemployment for Indians," concluded the report, adding that only casinos near major cities have thrived while "most others have little left after paying the bills."

"Poison Coming In"

None of this surprises Delores. "You always heard at village meetings, 'It's good money; look at all the money we are going to be getting from truck drivers and tourists,'" he says. "But in my heart I knew this was poison coming in."

And now he sees that poison in the faces of friends and neighbors—like the Laguna family living in a tiny brick and clay home tucked behind a windswept mesa. The mother, Cindy, stands at the kitchen window, gazing blankly at dust devils swirling outside. A physical therapist who works at the local hospital and supports three teenage daughters, she is obviously an intelligent woman. But Cindy can't figure out how to help her husband overcome his gambling addiction.

"I've tried everything; I've tried taking him to court . . . I've given him so many chances," she says. The final straw came a few nights ago when her husband lost yet another paycheck at the casino. They fought—hard—and Cindy decided to give up.

"I'm filing for divorce this week," she says, pointing out the window toward the Laguna Travel Center. "He just goes right down the road here. What they say is true; gambling breaks up families. He's lost all respect from the kids, and I lost all trust in him."

Outside, her husband, who declines to give his first name, is equally dejected. "I've got a good wife, healthy children, and they don't respect me anymore," he says, staring at the ground. "I can't describe it; it hurts too much."

It all started the night four years ago he won $5,000 at a casino. "It seems like after that I just can't quit. . . . I just blame myself," he says, never looking up as he rakes the yard with angry, jerking motions. "I don't know what's gotten into me. I'm not the same person anymore. The problem is, I know my paycheck's going to be there the next week."

A few feeble-minded addicts like this shouldn't be allowed to spoil gambling benefits for the whole tribe, argue casino backers who justify their profit-from-the-weakest philosophy by promising funding for addiction-recovery programs.

But gambling's social costs far outweigh any economic benefit, according to Navajo financial analyst Richard Kontz. While working for the Navajo Economic Development Division in 1997, he examined proposals for 10 on-site casinos and concluded they were a raw deal.

"They said they would create 3,000 jobs. But when you consider that unemployment is anywhere from 46 to 50 percent, to create 3,000 jobs from gambling would only reduce that rate by 1 percent. And yet think of all the headaches we would bring on—increased alcoholism, increased domestic abuse, increased child neglect. All those increased social problems and the cost of dealing with addicts—it doesn't balance out."

> **Parasitic casinos feeding off low-income families only deepen Navajo dependency on welfare.**

So why are government officials and tribe leaders still promoting it?

"It's not glamorous to say, 'I created 10 jobs in Pothole, New Mexico,'" explains Kontz. "It's easier for them to say, 'Hey, I created a $20 million casino.' It's a big, glitzy thing for them to point to as opposed to 10 jobs at 15 different businesses throughout the reservation—but that's what the Navajo people need."

An Unlikely Alliance

It's 11 A.M., and seated around a table at the Navajo Nation Inn restaurant, one of the reservation's only privately owned businesses, are a Navajo mom, the wife of a former tribe president convicted of taking bribes and the financial analyst who testified against him—Kontz.

It's an unlikely alliance forged around a common cause: opposition to gambling. "[Casinos] are making money at the expense of our souls, at the very fiber of Navajo being," says Wanda MacDonald, who oversees a government outpatient addiction treatment center.

In addition to escalating addiction, MacDonald (wife of the convicted tribe president) fears gambling will lead to fraud.

"The [Indian] leaders where you put that casino are wide

open to manipulation and corruption," she says, explaining that most Native Americans lack the experience to run million-dollar enterprises and must seek outside help that leaves them open to temptation. "Sad to say, we are just human beings, and it happens. It just gives someone else in the world a big profit . . . and it doesn't feed back into the community."

As a result, MacDonald and Kontz—the activist odd couple —have teamed up to spread the word about how gambling hurts their tribe.

Joining them is Karen Schell, a petite, soft-spoken Navajo mother of three, who heard Kontz speak at her church. "I thought, 'How can I get involved, do it at home and still get out information?'"

Then she met a missionary with a button maker. "Me and the kids made buttons up that said 'Dooda' [the Navajo word for 'no'] gaming,'" she says. "We had big envelopes and we stuffed about 20 in each of them and sent them to churches with a letter. . . . It said that as Christian Navajos they needed to know how gaming would affect our reservation."

Other activists, including Navajo lawyers and ministers, have joined Kontz and company, distributing fliers at reservation hearings, pitching in to pay for radio ads and holding community rallies near the Capitol. But with more pressure coming from Gov. Hull and some of their own tribe leaders, they wonder how much longer they can keep the monster at bay.

"To me it's a spiritual battle, and Satan is not going to quit," says Kontz. "He wants to destroy families, and he's going to keep coming from every angle—whether it be alcohol or gambling."

Back at the Navajo Council Chamber, Wauneka and his colleagues are discussing the same issue. Ironically, Wauneka sits beneath a mural of Indians industriously planting corn and hunting as he warns that parasitic casinos feeding off low-income families only deepen Navajo dependency on welfare. Then he refers back to The Gambler. "The prophecy was that he'll be back. So a lot of people say, 'What's the use of trying to go against it?'

"But I look at it differently. If we fight against it, if we unite to oppose gaming, I don't care if this is the prophecy or legend.

"The people can prevail."

11

Indian Gaming Offers a Therapeutic Escape to Many Senior Citizens

Dave McKibben

Dave McKibben is a staff writer for the Los Angeles Times.

Many senior citizens are spending their retirement years playing slot machines and other games at Indian casinos. At a time in their lives when they often suffer from the loss of spouses and relentless boredom, retirees are finding that casinos provide stimulation and excitement. The attraction to Indian casinos benefits not only the tribes but the seniors who play their games. Studies have shown that older gamblers are in better health than nongamblers. Although some experts caution that gambling addiction can be a serious problem for seniors, casinos cater to their older clientele, offering bus services from retirement communities to the casinos. For some elderly people, Indian casinos add an element of joy not found elsewhere in their lives.

I t's barely noon, and 78-year-old Rose Kario is already $300 in the hole. With each puff of her cigarette and each losing spin, she grows more agitated.

"Come on, sweetie pie," she whispers to a clanging slot machine she has been feeding for more than an hour at Casino Pauma in northern San Diego County. "Come to Mama."

A few minutes later, Kario's patience is gone. She swears as another spin comes up empty.

Two seats over, 80-year-old Clara Stern isn't having much luck either. But as she watches the last of her $200 in credits spin away, Stern says she is getting her money's worth.

Cost what it may—and gambling has cost her plenty—the casino visit is a welcome respite from what for her is the monotony of old age.

"I have no limit," Stern says in a voice husky from years of chain-smoking. "I don't know if I'm going to wake up tomorrow."

A Growing Number of Seniors

Kario and Stern are among thousands of senior citizens in California who have become regular customers of the state's growing number of Indian casinos, which now look to the elderly for half their business, experts say. Casinos actively encourage the trend by dispatching fleets of buses to retirement communities and senior centers and by offering incentives such as buffet vouchers.

The trend reflects a national pattern: A study by the federal National Gambling Impact Study Commission in 1999 found that the fraction of U.S. seniors who gambled jumped from 20% in 1974 to 50% in 1998, a surge unmatched by any other age group during a period when casinos proliferated across the country.

It's still unclear, however, what easy access to casino gambling means for senior citizens in California, where Native American tribes have opened 54 casinos jammed with as many as 60,000 slot machines.

> *Many retirees say casinos have improved the quality of their lives by providing a change of pace and intellectual stimulation.*

Although some experts worry about gambling addictions, many retirees say casinos have improved the quality of their lives by providing a change of pace and intellectual stimulation.

"We're not interested in sitting home and watching TV every day," said Phyllis Zalomek, 82, who arrived at Casino Pauma on a chartered bus from Leisure World in Laguna Woods along with

Kario, Stern and about 50 others. "It's a place to go, a place to occupy your mind."

Experts on gambling and aging agree with many senior gamblers that casinos do offer a change of scene that is attractive—even, perhaps, beneficial.

"Seniors are often dealing with loss of a spouse, loneliness, boredom, or they are unable to cope with retirement. For all those reasons, casinos can be a very comfortable place for seniors," said Bruce Roberts, president of the California Council on Problem Gambling.

One recent study concluded that recreational gamblers older than 65 reported better overall health than their non-gambling peers. The social, physical and cognitive stimulation of gambling could be part of the reason, said Yale epidemiologist Rani Desai, one of the study authors.

> *Recreational gamblers older than 65 reported better overall health than their non-gambling peers.*

It also could simply be that "among the older folks, gamblers are healthier to begin with,"—healthy enough to go to casinos, Desai said.

Despite the potential benefits, many experts say gambling addictions are being kindled—with unforeseeable consequences for retirees and their families.

"Ever since the growth of Indian casinos, so many more seniors are gambling away their golden years," said Suzanne Graupner Pike, a psychologist with the San Diego Center for Pathological Gambling. "It's tragic."

No hard statistics are available, but seniors are just as vulnerable as younger people to gambling problems, they say, and the proliferation of casinos inevitably will ruin lives.

Pike, who has been treating gamblers for 11 years, said one-third of her nearly 50 patients are seniors, and each is hooked on gambling at Indian casinos. Several of her elderly patients have refinanced their homes to pay off gambling debts, some have filed for bankruptcy and a few have attempted suicide, she said.

"Aging is a time of repeated losses, and that can lead to depression," said Pike, who gets most of her referrals from a Gamblers Anonymous toll-free hotline. "Seniors are separating from their children geographically and losing their sense of self through retirement. So they go to the casinos to escape from their lives."

Casinos welcome retirees with enthusiasm—in part because they arrive during the day, when other gamblers are scarce.

"Seniors are half the market of Indian casinos," said Bill Thompson, a University of Nevada-Las Vegas professor of public administration who has written nine books on gambling. "They are the perfect demographic for the casinos."

Kathy Swank, a spokeswoman for Harrah's Rincon, another north San Diego County casino, agreed. "Seniors are a great market for us," said Swank, who said her casino did 42% of its September business with adults older than 60. "They have more discretionary income and more time on their hands," Swank said. "During the week, the seniors and the bus program support us."

To keep the seniors coming, Harrah's and other casinos pay independent bus operators to maintain elaborate schedules, funneling in retirees from throughout Southern California. In September alone, 12 Harrah's buses carried more than 32,000 people—80% of them older than 60—to the casino.

> *The seniors descend . . . on the slot machines—and stay there all day.*

One of those buses goes to south Orange County's Leisure World [retirement community] every weekday, arriving at 6 A.M. and returning by dinnertime. Two other Indian casinos each send buses to the retirement community once a week.

In addition, the largest social organization at Leisure World, the Players Club, charters buses to casinos on average three times a week. The group used to offer mostly trips to the theater. Today, its 400 loyal members mostly go to casinos and gamble.

About 50 Players Club members are visiting Casino Pauma on this recent trip. At 10 A.M., they are nearly alone in the dark dome-shaped building off California 76 in an empty, wooded patch of northern San Diego County.

There is a long wooden bar and tables for blackjack, poker, pai gow, roulette and craps. But most of them are empty, their dealers waiting quietly. The seniors descend instead on the slot machines—and stay there all day.

Among them are Kario and Stern, both dedicated gamblers who visit casinos as much as three times a week. Unlike most of the others from Leisure World, they also travel regularly to Laughlin, Nev., and Las Vegas—where Stern, in particular, likes to play poker, blackjack and craps in addition to the slots.

Stern and Kario are not only the highest rollers among the Leisure World group, they're also the most dapper. While much of the crowd is dressed in sweat shirts and tennis shoes, Stern is wearing white slacks and a red blouse, Kario an expensive tan suit.

By 2 P.M., Kario, Stern and three friends have decided it's finally time for lunch. But no one really feels like eating. Sitting at a table outside the casino coffee shop, they nibble on eclairs, cake and tarts, smoke cigarettes and reminisce.

After lunch, Stern and Kario begin to cut their losses and move to the quarter slots. Stern's luck doesn't improve, so she tries using her feet to tap the button.

A few minutes later, restless, she gets up and does a little dance, slowly twirling, laughing and waving her arms. The movement helps loosen up her arthritic right leg. But it doesn't change her fortunes.

Looking for some comic relief, Stern approaches a cocktail waitress. "Honey, are you with the casino?" she says. "Can you fix this machine? It's taking all my money."

Stern considers casinos her sanctuary. Stern, a twice-widowed survivor of Auschwitz, flees her Laguna Woods condominium three days a week for the comfort of the Indian casinos.

She says she doesn't know or care how much she's lost over the years but acknowledges that she refinanced her Leisure World condo this year to pay off gambling debts.

Susan Conforti, Stern's daughter, believes that casinos are therapeutic and enthusiastically approves of her mother's habit.

Her two sisters "think she's gambling away their inheritance," Conforti said. "But my mom has had a really rotten life. And if the slot machines are a legal way of numbing yourself, I say go for it."

That's how Stern sees it. "I have such a sad past," she says, taking a drag from a cigarette with her left hand and playfully pounding the dollar slot machine with her right. "This is my enjoyment."

12

Casinos Hurt Local Businesses

Jonathan Krutz

Jonathan Krutz is on the Gambling with the Good Life's board of directors. Gambling with the Good Life is a grass-roots citizen-action organization formed to oppose expanded Indian gaming in the state of Nebraska in order to preserve what they describe as the "Good Life."

Supporters of Indian gaming often brag that casinos bring prosperity to the surrounding community. The facts speak otherwise, however. Studies and surveys have shown that casinos cause small businesses to suffer, increase crime and bankruptcy, and place an extra burden on police departments. Indian casinos drain money from the community at the expense of local hotels, restaurants, taverns, and other enterprises. Considering as well the misery suffered by problem gamblers and their families, Indian gaming comes at a price most communities cannot afford.

Each of South Dakota's 8,000 video slots takes an average of $13,750 in consumer spending annually out of the local economy, according to a Deloitte Touche report. If the devices were not there, South Dakota would have "... a $105.4 million spending injection into the economy." "Chubb Foods experienced a 15% drop in retail sales after the casino boats opened in Council Bluffs [Iowa]. That is a small loss compared to the heartache gambling causes to individuals and families," said Ron Meredith, owner of the North Omaha grocery store.

Jonathan Krutz, MBA, "Gambling's Impact on the Business Community," www.gamblingwiththegoodlife.com, September 8, 2004. Copyright © 2004 by Gambling with the Good Life. Reproduced by permission.

Bankruptcy Increases

Bankruptcy rates in U.S. counties with casinos are 18% higher than those without casinos, according to a banking industry study. [According to the 1999 National Gambling Impact Study Commission Report,] "Nineteen percent of Chapter 13 bankruptcies in the State of Iowa involved gambling-related debt. Bankruptcies in Iowa increased at a rate significantly above the national average in the years following the introduction of casinos."

> *Bankruptcy rates in U.S. counties with casinos are 18% higher than those without casinos.*

"[B]usinesses in communities which initiate legalized gambling activities can anticipate increased personnel costs due to increased job absenteeism and declining productivity. The best blue-collar and white-collar workers, the Type-A personalities, are the most likely to become pathological gamblers. A business with 1,000 workers can anticipate increased personnel costs of $500,000 or more per year—simply by having various forms of legalized gambling activities accessible to its workers," said University of Illinois Professor John Kindt in sworn testimony to Congress.

Increased Crime

"In a survey of nearly 400 Gamblers Anonymous members, 57 percent admitted stealing to finance their gambling. Collectively, they stole $30 million, for an average of $135,000 per individual" [reported University of Illinois Professor Henry Lesieur].

More Problem Gamblers

Between 1989 and 1995, Iowa's problem gambler rate jumped from 1.7% to 5.4%. If video slots across Nebraska have just half that impact (a 1.85% jump), 30,000 more Nebraskans would become problem gamblers. In 1995, Omaha's Open Door Mission (before the casinos opened in Council Bluffs) had 11% of their homeless clients as a result of gambling. In 2003 it was

35%. These are the men and women who attribute gambling addiction to their becoming homeless.

Increased Business and Taxpayer Costs Due to Problem Gamblers

Estimates of problem gambler costs for bankruptcies, fraud, embezzlement, unpaid debts, and increased criminal justice expenses range from $13,200 to $52,000/year. At $13,200, 30,000 new problem gamblers in Nebraska would cost $396 million.

Harm to Business

In a survey of 900 Minnesota restaurant owners, 38 percent said they had lost business due to gambling. Only 10 percent reported an increase in business due to the existence of casinos. . . .

The number of retail businesses in Gilpin County, Colorado, dropped from 31 before gambling to 11 within a couple of years after casinos arrived. Gilpin County is home to the majority of the state's casinos.

More than 70 percent of businesses in Natchez, Mississippi, reported declining sales within a few months of the opening of that city's first riverboat [casino].

More than half of business owners in Illinois riverboat casino towns reported either a negative effect or no effect on their businesses from the presence of casinos. Only 3 percent of respondents said their businesses had been "helped a lot" by the casinos.

A University of South Dakota study showed that retail and service businesses in South Dakota suffered a net loss of approximately $60 million in anticipated sales in the year following the introduction of gambling.

13

Indian Casinos Generate Crime and Corruption

Clara NiiSka

Clara NiiSka is a journalist who frequently writes articles for the Ojibwe News.

Casinos have been immensely profitable for some Indian tribes but these profits come at a high social cost. Wherever casinos are found, there are major increases in crime, bankruptcy, and other ills. Casino-related criminal activities include bank robbery, car theft, embezzlement, prostitution, and drug trafficking. Supporters of Indian casinos argue that the profits generated by these businesses help to compensate for the injustices Native Americans have suffered. However, the social costs of these casinos outstrip any benefits.

G overnment-owned gambling enterprises, whether Indian casinos or a state-owned casino, seem like a good way for the government to raise money. No new taxes, just "vending machines" (slot machines) selling the hope of "winning big" and pouring revenue into state and tribal coffers. "If you don't want to spend money on gambling, don't gamble," we are told. Voluntary contributions subsidizing the government is a wonderful idea . . . isn't it?

The National Gambling Impact Study Commission (NGISC) was established by Congress in 1996, and released its official reports three years later, recommended a national moratorium of

the expansion of gambling, and more study of the costs, benefits and effects of gambling.

There have been subsequent studies of the effects of gambling, including articles published last summer [2001] in the
academic journal *Managerial and Decision Economics*, which devoted a full issue to consideration of gambling and its consequences.

The academic paper, "Business Profitability versus Social
Profitability: Evaluating Industries with Externalities, the Case
of Casinos," was co-authored by economists Earl L. Grinols and
David B. Mustard. Using an econometric cost-benefit analysis,
these economists found that, "the costs of casinos are at least
1.9 times greater than the benefits." In other words, a dollar
worth of casino profits—and other social benefits—costs taxpayers at least $1.90: in "cost-creating activities such as crime,
suicide, and bankruptcy," and in the expensive social problems
engendered by 'problem and pathological' gamblers.

Casinos Create Crime

In an earlier paper, "Casinos, Crime, and Community Costs,"
Grinols, Mustard, and their fellow economist Cynthia Hunt
Dilley concluded that, "casinos increase crime in their host
counties and that crime spills over into neighboring counties
to increase crime in border areas."

> *A dollar worth of casino profits . . . costs
> taxpayers at least $1.90: 'in cost-creating activities
> such as crime, suicide, and bankruptcy.'*

Grinols, Mustard, and Dilley analyzed county crime rates for
every U.S. county between 1977 and 1996. "Casinos create
crime, rather than attract[ing] it from elsewhere," they found. In
1996, the last year for which statistics were available at the time
of their study, "casinos accounted for 10.3 percent of violent
crime, and 7.7 percent of property crime in casino counties."
Auto theft is the crime that increased the most as a result of casinos; robberies increased by 20%, despite increased expenditures
by law enforcement agencies after the casinos opened.

The data shows a time-lag between casino opening and

higher crime rates, which typically begin a few years after casinos open and increase over time. The researchers theorized that much of that time-lag reflected the addictive processes of 'problem and pathological gamblers,' who "according to clinical research, take two or three years to exhaust alternative resources before they commit crime.". . . .

Press/ON [Native American Press/Ojibwe News] contacted Earl Grinols and David Mustard, and asked them about their research. Both economists said that their published assessments of the costs of casinos were "conservative," and that inclusion of other less-measurable factors would establish that the social and other costs of casinos are even higher.

> // 'Corruption is a statistical certainty' in the gambling industry. //

"A lot of social costs are hidden, not easily observed," said Mustard. Some crimes in particular are harder to measure accurately, for example prostitution, he said.

Grinols put it bluntly to Press/ON: "We found that casinos are making crime." He explained that casinos create problems for pathological gamblers, and also that the "concentration of people with money is an 'attractive nuisance' to criminal activities. . . . Also, it might be that casinos change the social fabric—the 'get rich quick mentality'."

He also pointed out that "corruption is a statistical certainty" in the gambling industry, and that problems of corruption are exacerbated with respect to Indian casinos because of the jurisdictional ambiguities in which they are entangled. Grinols said, "The regulatory agency is often captured by the industry they are supposed to regulate." He also commented that in at least one state, "the gambling industry 'owns' the legislature.". . .

Casino-Related Crime in Minnesota?

In their paper, "Casinos, Crime, and Community Costs," economists Grinols, Mustard and Dilley present compelling documentation that casinos do, in fact, increase crime. Their published analysis draws on nationwide statistics. Have crime rates in Minnesota followed the same pattern? Have Minnesota's Indian casinos fueled a crime wave? . . .

Minnesota's increases in crime—both in counties with casinos and in neighboring "collar counties"—follow a pattern strikingly similar to that found by Grinols, Mustard and Dilley in their nationwide study: after a time lag, crime rose and in some instances crime rates soared.

Press/ON discussed the results of our analysis with two criminal justice officials who have previous experience with the gambling industry. Both confirmed that the statistics fit with what they had observed 'in the field,' and added their own off-the-record anecdotal observations.

Press/ON asked about the dynamics of the interrelationships between casinos and increased crime. Do problem and pathological gamblers account for all of the problem, we wondered, or does the 'time lag' followed by sharply increased crime rates also reflect the development of a criminal infrastructure associated with casinos? One of the officials detailed his observations of the casino-related drug trade in support of our criminal-infrastructure theory. The other less directly confirmed the connections between casinos and homegrown criminal organization, but stressed the sometime spectacular bank robberies, embezzlements, and other crimes committed by compulsive gamblers.

It is clear, however, that there has been a significant increase in crime correlated with casinos. And, as David Mustard told Press/ON, it is also clear that "externalities"—the costs associated with casinos—must be considered along with the benefits which gambling proponents claim come from government-operated gambling enterprises. "There are more things we need to find out . . . to get people, neutral parties, to think about seriously," he said.

Earl Grinols summed it up, "Gambling is a loser from society's point of view. . . . It's what my research leads me to. . . . The costs exceed the benefits, 1.9 to 1, and that's a conservative estimate. . . . Gambling carries with it social costs" that outweigh the benefits. "I think that most people, when they hear that casinos are owned by Indians, say, 'that is great'," it helps compensate for the injustices of the past and provides badly-needed money for impoverished Indian tribes. But, he said, "we need to recognize that this vehicle is harmful to society as a whole." We need to look at the whole picture.

14

Christian Activists Are Fighting to Stop the Creation of More Indian Casinos

John W. Kennedy

John W. Kennedy is news editor of Today's Pentecostal
Evangel, *the weekly magazine of the Assemblies of God and
the most widely read Pentecostal magazine in the world.*

The rapid growth of Indian casinos in California has led
to increased gambling addiction, rising crime, and broken families. With more tribes gaining official government recognition, and others building casinos far from
their reservations, Evangelical Christians need to come
together to fight gambling expansion at a local level.
While the struggle against these financial giants may be
difficult, communities will benefit if religious people
oppose the construction of more Indian casinos.

With the blessing of his 145-member Assemblies of God
congregation in Barstow, California, pastor Charles Mattix III has become a community activist. He has lobbied in the
nation's capital, spoken at city council meetings, encouraged
residents to sign petitions, helped organize a community forum
attended by more than 500 residents, and formed an ad-hoc responsible growth coalition. His cause? Mattix opposes a proposed casino to be operated by the Los Coyotes of the Cahuilla
tribe.

[In 2000] California voters approved a constitutional amendment that gave tribes a monopoly on operating casinos in California, as long as they do so on tribal land. Now, Barstow is just one of 28 "off-reservation" casino proposals in the Golden State.

On June 21, [2004,] Gov. Arnold Schwarzenegger signed a deal with five tribes that would allow unlimited slot machines—the current limit is 2,000 per tribe—for $1 billion and a share of future revenues. Foes say such an accord, combined with approval of more off-reservation casinos, would result in American Indian gambling inundating urban areas such as Los Angeles and San Francisco—making gambling a significant feature of California life.

Although the 272-member Los Coyotes already control 25,000 acres in rural mountains near San Diego, they consider the cacti, rocks, sand, and sagebrush on the edge of Barstow the perfect locale for a casino. Barstow, a city of 23,000, is on Interstate 15 in the Mojave Desert, roughly midway between Los Angeles and Las Vegas, a spot passed by 19.3 million vehicles annually.

"I fear that the casino will become the plantation and the city of Barstow its slaves," Mattix says. "Families would split, credit card debt would rise, crime would increase, and there would be more drug addiction."

More than 40 local pastors signed a letter to the city council outlining moral and social problems the casino would cause. Pastors gather for an hour each week to pray for the community—and for each other.

For decades churches have been fighting a losing battle against gambling interests. The latest front is Indian casinos, a rapidly growing national phenomenon that earns as much revenue as Atlantic City gambling. Despite the onslaught, some Christians, like those in Barstow, have refused to give up the struggle.

Placing Their Bets

[In 1988] Congress passed the Indian Gaming Regulatory Act (IGRA), which regulates tribal gambling on reservations. Tribal casinos are big business. There are 369 tribal gambling operations in 29 states. California, with 56, has the most. Because casinos are on sovereign tribal land, they are exempt from federal, state, and local taxes. In 2001, a total of 200 tribal casinos grossed $12.7 billion of legal gambling's annual $30 billion in revenue, and tribes kept $5 billion as profit.

The United States has 601 federal- or state-recognized tribes, but another 200 want to reorganize, many because they want to cash in on the gambling windfall. Payoffs can make tribes with a few dozen members wealthy in a hurry.

Congress designed IGRA to alleviate poverty. But nearly 80 percent of American Indians receive no financial benefit from gambling revenues, according to U.S. Rep. Frank R. Wolf (R-Va.).

> *I fear that the casino will become the plantation and the city of Barstow its slaves.*

Wolf claims the process of officially recognizing legitimate tribes has become corrupted because of the money gambling investors have poured into helping defunct tribes gain legal standing. Guy C. Clark, chairman of the National Coalition Against Gambling Expansion (NCAGE), wrote to President [George W.] Bush in January [2004], charging that the Bureau of Indian Affairs is granting official recognition to American Indian groups with dubious historical claims.

In February, Wolf called for Secretary of the Interior Gale Norton to suspend approvals and launch an investigation of the bureau for possible irregularities in "exploiting Indians and potentially corrupting government officials."

The NCAGE has made Indian casino expansion its 2004 focus precisely because of the "reservation shopping" done by gambling investors, says Tom Gray, NCAGE executive director and a United Methodist minister in Rockford, Illinois. "The fact that casinos now can move off reservations violates the spirit of IGRA."

Many small cities and towns, though, aren't all that concerned about a tribe's legitimacy or the spirit of IGRA. For first-term Barstow mayor Lawrence E. Dale, the key issue is creating jobs.

"We're not turning away anything that will bring jobs, and the casino would bring over 1,600 jobs," Dale says at Barstow's city hall. City officials frame the debate by pitting those who want economic progress against those who don't. First-year revenues at the casino, backed by developer BarWest Gaming, are projected at $175 million. Barstow contains several empty and boarded-up businesses, including Sears, JCPenney, Kmart, and Yellow Freight.

In fact, casinos do make a difference to some economies. Doug Elmets, spokesman for the United Auburn tribe and the Thunder Valley Casino outside of Sacramento, says the newly opened casino employs 2,000 people and pumps $30 million annually into the economy through vendor contracts. Immediately after the casino opened, the 255 members of the tribe received medical insurance, dental coverage, and vision care, plus a pension program, Elmets says.

Facts like these make the struggle against Indian casinos harder for many.

Mobilizing the Laity

A few blocks from the state capitol in Sacramento, five Christian activists met on a Monday morning to plot strategy. They gathered at an inner-city United Methodist church where Harvey Chinn, an NCAGE member, is on staff.

The glue that holds the anti-gambling forces together is Cheryl Schmit, director of Stand Up for California, a grassroots watchdog group. Schmit is a former librarian at a Catholic high school. She became an activist a few years ago when the 247-member United Auburn Indian tribe—which had disbanded 40 years earlier—received congressional recognition and planned to open its casino within a mile of her home in Penryn. Thirty miles north of Sacramento along I-80, Penryn has 2,000 residents and a median income of $30,000.

> *The Bureau of Indian Affairs is granting official recognition to American Indian groups with dubious historical claims.*

Schmit convinced Placer County officials to move the 1,900-slot Thunder Valley casino to a less obtrusive location.

The casino opened a year ago off Highway 65 north of the Sacramento suburb of Rocklin, far from residential areas. Cows and a sanitary landfill are the closest neighbors. Schmit also ensured that casino operators, rather than taxpayers, paid for street and sewer installation.

Schmit now travels the state advising community groups on how to confront cities seeking casino revenue—and giving hope to discouraged activists.

Yuba County Supervisor Dan Logue assumed office in 2001 and opposes a casino that the board of supervisors had approved before his election.

"This casino will be built only if the body of Christ allows it," Logue says in his real-estate office in Linda, outside Marysville in northern California. "God laid it upon my heart to make this issue my highest priority."

But waging the battle alone wore down Logue, a Foursquare Gospel church member. His blood pressure skyrocketed and one of his kidneys failed. Logue, 53, was about to pack it in when he met Schmit, who lent her organizational expertise. "This woman has high-powered lobbyists trembling," says Logue, who has a portrait of Abraham Lincoln on one wall of his office and a picture of John Wayne on another. "Without Cheryl, this casino would have been built by now."

> *This casino will be built only if the body of Christ allows it. . . . God laid it upon my heart to make this issue my highest priority.*

A group of Yuba County evangelical pastors started meeting to pray for Logue. He no longer needs a kidney transplant.

The approved casino that Logue and others are fighting would belong to the 215-member Enterprise Rancheria Tribe. It has its sights set on a Highway 65 location only 25 miles north of Sacramento, an area expected to boom in the next five years. The tribe is based 45 miles north in Oroville—but that city of 13,000 already has two casinos. . . .

"If we do nothing, we will lose." Logue says, "These guys already own the state government. The only place to stop them is at the local level."

Battle of Attrition

An entity dubbed the Federated Indians of Graton Rancheria, 568 people from the Miwoks and Pamos tribes, had no federal government recognition until 2000. With congressional recognition came a federal guarantee of a gambling site. And because the tribe has no land, it is allowed to buy a casino site.

The Graton Rancheria group eventually set its sights on Rohnert Park, a city of 42,000 people, 40 miles north of San Francisco. In stark contrast to the high desert of Barstow, Rohnert Park is in the verdant rolling hills of Sonoma County wine country.

Chip Worthington, who has been pastor of Rohnert Park Assembly of God for a quarter-century, traveled to Washington last September [2003]. He met with members of Congress and White House and Department of Justice staff, and delivered petitions signed by 4,700 residents.

Despite his efforts, the city council voted 4-1 the next month to approve construction of a tribal hotel and casino complex on 360 acres on the city's outskirts.

But Worthington believes he can so frustrate the developers that they will look elsewhere. Worthington filed suit in November [2003] against the city of Rohnert Park and Station Casinos, the casino's financial backer, arguing for an environmental study. Worthington filed another suit in December, demanding that residents be allowed to vote on the casino. In April [2004] a county judge dismissed one lawsuit, ruling that an environmental study could come later.

Other Rohnert Park protesters have launched a recall movement against four city council members who sanctioned gambling. On a Friday afternoon, Lynne Conde, who attends Rohnert Park Bible Church, is in front of the local Roger Wilko Market looking for signatures. Says the homeschooling mom, who hopes to recall three council members: "God has called us to get out of our churches, put on our full armor, and walk through this thing."

15

Anti-Casino Groups Threaten Tribal Economics

Tom Wanamaker

Tom Wanamaker is a staff reporter who has written more than sixty-five articles for Indian Country Today.

In the twentieth century, dozens of Indian tribes lost federal recognition when the government sought to assimilate tribe members into white society. With this loss of recognition, the tribes could no longer receive federal protection, services, and benefits, such as sovereignty, available to Indian tribes by virtue of their status as tribes. As the casino business continues to boom, however, more Indians are hoping to regain federal tribal recognition so that they too can open gambling establishments. In Connecticut, antigaming forces oppose the recognition of several indigenous tribes, therefore denying their right to exist as a people. This opposition is having a deleterious effect on hundreds of Native Americans whose official recognition by the federal government is long overdue.

Casinos and other types of gaming, particularly lotteries, have flourished over the past several years as more and more states look to remedy fiscal maladies in their budgets. Concerns over the social problems stereotypically associated with gambling—crime, drugs, prostitution and compulsive addiction as well as issues of the "morality" of gambling, often provoke a knee-jerk, anti-gaming reaction from many otherwise reasonable people. Add in the Indian factor, with which usually comes a lack of understanding by the general public of the nature and roots of Indian sovereignty, and you're left with people who rabidly oppose something they may not completely understand and may not have a viable alternative for. The Indian gaming controversies in Connecticut . . . visibly illustrate this phenomenon.

Vivid Backlash

The recent federal recognition of the historic Eastern Pequot Tribe combined the Paucatuck Eastern Pequot and the Eastern Pequot factions, who had sought recognition well before Indian country's casino explosion. Their joint recognition ignited a vivid backlash of anti-casino sentiment throughout Connecticut. The state attorney general [Richard Blumenthal] has indicated he will appeal the decision, as have the towns surrounding the tribe's Lantern Hill reservation and other anti-casino activist groups. The fact that other Connecticut tribes, including the Golden Hill Paugussetts and the Schagticokes, are seeking recognition and possibly casinos has even further fanned the anti-gaming flames.

> *[Casino opponents] rabidly oppose something they may not completely understand and may not have a viable alternative for.*

Connecticut already boasts two Indian casinos, which just happen to be two of the most successful gaming operations in Indian country. The Mashantucket Pequots' Foxwoods Casino and the Mohegan Tribe's Mohegan Sun have both, under terms of their compacts, contributed millions of dollars to the state of Connecticut over the years. Curiously, the state divides this money among its municipalities based upon their population; thus bigger cities like Bridgeport and Hartford receive considerably more cash than do the smaller casino-adjacent towns that actually bear the brunt of such things like extra traffic and burgeoning school enrollments. Perhaps this flawed formula contributes to some of the local hostility toward the casinos.

Appeals for Federal Recognition

On Aug. 23 [2002], there emerged a rather unlikely challenger to the historic Easterns. The *Day*, a newspaper in New London [CT], reported that the Wiquapaug Eastern Pequot Tribe, based in Hope Valley, R.I., said that it plans to file an appeal of the historic Easterns' recognition. The 119-member tribe, which according to the AP [Associated Press] was forced off the Lantern Hill reservation in the 1800s, claims to be the true descendant of the Eastern Pequot tribe.

> *In order to prevent tribes from building casinos, they attack recognition and tribal legitimacy, in effect denying that tribe's existence as a people.*

The Wiquapaugs had filed for status as an "interested party" in the BIA's [Bureau of Indian Affairs] original recognition of the two factions (Paucatucks and Easterns). A BIA spokesman told the AP, however, that the Wiquapaug's own recognition application, filed in September 2000, was incomplete, which was probably why the group was not included in the historic Eastern Pequot recognition.

Unfortunately for the Connecticut tribes (federally recognized or not) that do not yet have a casino, prospects for entering the gaming community seem to be a long way off. The historic Eastern Pequots, and the Golden Hill Paugussetts, if they do get recognized, will undoubtedly face a myriad of appeals, lawsuits and other litigious action aimed at depriving them of possible economic self-determination. These tribes have the double misfortune of not only living in a densely populated, highly trafficked state, but also of following the Mohegans' and Mashantuckets' wildly successful casinos.

Many of the anti-casino people claim that they are not against the tribes themselves; they say they only oppose the prospect of more casinos. But in order to prevent tribes from building casinos, they attack recognition and tribal legitimacy, in effect denying that tribe's existence as a people. And these attacks come, in the historic Easterns' case, despite the fact that Connecticut itself, the Colony of Connecticut, established

Lantern Hill in 1683, a move predating the formation of the United States.

While gaming is certainly not a panacea, it has become the most successful means of economic self-determination throughout Indian country. If Connecticut's anti-casino crowd is genuinely concerned about the welfare of the state's tribes, perhaps they might suggest some viable economic alternatives to casinos that will allow tribes to house, educate, employ and provide medical care for their members.

16

Many Indian Gaming Opponents Are Biased Against Native Americans

Zoltan Grossman and Debra McNutt

Zoltan Grossman and Debra McNutt are members of the Midwest Treaty Network, an alliance that supports Native American sovereignty. Grossman is an assistant professor of geography and American Indian Studies at the University of Wisconsin–Eau Claire. McNutt is a longtime antiracism and environmental activist.

When white business owners donate millions to influence elections, they rarely face public criticism. Unfortunately, Native Americans are held to a different standard. Indians playing big-money politics have been maligned in national news sources and by antitribal gaming organizations. Now that a few tribes have been able to profit from the casino boom, critics should applaud their success. To do otherwise implies that what is acceptable for white people is not acceptable for Indians.

From coast to coast, the new front for the movement against Native American sovereignty is renewed opposition to Indian gaming. In New York state, anti-Indian groups have strongly opposed Oneida casinos that fund the tribe's land claims. In California, Arnold Schwarzenegger used his opposition to Indian gaming compacts as a central plank in his campaign for governor [in 2003]. In Wisconsin, although tribal casinos have been largely accepted in the north, they are being challenged in Madison. Wherever it has surfaced in the country, the opposition to Indian casinos often exhibits a racial double standard, by focusing its efforts on Indian gaming, while ignoring or even supporting non-Indian gaming interests.

> *The message is unmistakably clear: it is fine for the white majority to profit from gaming, but it is somehow scandalous for a minority group to benefit.*

Under the 1988 Indian Gaming Regulatory Act, tribes can have a level of gaming only within the same "class" as the state where it resides. Under this federal law, Wisconsin tribes can have Class III casinos[1] only because the State has a Class III lottery. But few activist groups or newspaper articles are focusing on the omnipresent lottery, illegal video poker in taverns, or other non-Indian gambling institutions.

The message is unmistakably clear: it is fine for the white majority to profit from gaming, but it is somehow scandalous for a minority group to benefit. Implications of the double standard do not have to be directly stated, just as police do not have to make "racist" comments when they selectively enforce drug laws along racial lines.

A few "anti-gambling" groups do strongly oppose gambling for moral or economic reasons, and focus consistently on all forms of gaming. But most groups (such as the Tavern League and the Donald Trump Group) spend no energy or money on opposing non-Indian gambling, but only challenge Indian casinos. Sincere anti-gambling citizens join such alliances, often unaware that they are allying with non-indian gambling interests against Indian competitors.

Anti-Gaming Rhetoric

Whites are generally not criticized for gaining wealth from a lucrative industry. Yet somehow, Native Americans are expected

1. A designation that includes all forms of "Nevada-style" gaming, including blackjack, craps, and slot machines.

to play by different rules, and not to lobby or contribute to politicians as white groups have done for decades. [California] Gov. Schwarzenegger, for example, criticized his election opponents [in 2003] for accepting donations from Indian tribes. The national anti-Indian network Citizens Equal Rights Alliance (CERA) criticizes [Wisconsin's] governor for accepting tribal donations, contending that "Wisconsin's tribes are very happy with new governor James Doyle . . . the rest of the State of Wisconsin is wondering who owns the new governor?" Anti-gaming rhetoric around the country is marked by remarkably similar hysteria that "the Indians" are taking over the state's politics or economy.

> *The truth is that most tribes are heavily in debt, cutting budgets, and still being shaken down by state governments.*

The face of anti-Indian prejudice has changed since the treaty rights conflict of the late 1980s. Back then, Indian-bashing was directed against a "poor" minority, using the type of prejudice previously reserved for African Americans. In the 2000s, Indian-bashing is directed against a supposedly "rich" minority, using the type of prejudice previously reserved for Jews. Like European Jews, Native Americans have developed particular financial industries because they have been denied control over land, and left with other few economic options open to them. And like the myth of the "Rich Jew," the myth of the "Rich Indian" implies that all tribal members are swimming in money. The truth is that most tribes are heavily in debt, cutting budgets, and still being shaken down by state governments.

Working with Neighbors

In the 1980s, Indians were bashed for being on welfare, now they are being bashed for getting off welfare. The tribes have also reduced welfare caseloads and funded programs for their neighboring communities. Tribes are now the largest employers (of Indians and non-Indians alike) in at least eight Wisconsin counties, even employing some former anti-treaty protesters. Some Wisconsin communities are learning about the tribal economies, and learning from them. Previously hostile white "border towns" near the reservations (Shawano, Minocqua, Crandon, Hayward, Green Bay, etc.) now recognize the benefits of nearby casinos to their own communities. The reservations used to be dependent on these "border towns," but now the dependency is mutual.

In 1997, when [former Wisconsin] Governor [Tommy] Thompson tried to blackmail the tribes into weakening their treaty rights and environmental regulations in return for gaming compacts, the tribes' Republican neighbors told him they needed the casino jobs and revenue sharing. In 2003, the neighbors of the Mole Lake Chippewa and Forest County Potawatomi were grateful that gaming revenue enabled these tribes to purchase the [polluting] Crandon mine site, and end the environmental threat to the local tourism industry. This victory was made possible not only by money, but by the cultural resurgence of the tribes, their political sovereignty, and their willingness to work with their neighbors. Yet this positive use of gaming revenue was quickly followed by opposition to a proposed Ho-Chunk casino in Madison.

The Ho-Chunk Nation has also been involved in environmental protection . . . and for land reclamation and bison restoration. Yet many Wisconsin citizens seem to only think of "Ho-Chunk" as a casino, rather than an ancient culture with a long history of resistance to ethnic cleansing from our state. . . . [The Ho Chunk have been] the poorest group in southern Wisconsin, with substandard housing and medical care. Revenue from three casinos has enabled the Ho-Chunk to finally develop their economy, yet the tribe has born the brunt of ridicule for its efforts. . . .

A Wisconsin citizen can be critical of gambling, but nonetheless support the tribes' right to use their sovereignty to strive toward economic equality. In response to the renewed conflict between Indian and non-Indian communities, peace and justice activists can support cooperation that protects the local environment and economy from corporate interests.

Organizations to Contact

The editors have compiled the following list of organizations concerned with the issues debated in this book. The descriptions are derived from materials provided by the organizations. All have publications or information available for interested readers. The list was compiled on the date of publication of the present volume; the information provided here may change. Be aware that many organizations take several weeks or longer to respond to inquiries, so allow as much time as possible.

American Indian Movement (AIM)
PO Box 13521, Minneapolis, MN 55414
(612) 724-3129 • fax: (612) 724-8090
e-mail: AIMGGC@worldnet.att.net • Web site: www.aimovement.org

Since 1973 the American Indian Movement has organized Native American communities and created opportunities for indigenous people across the Americas and Canada. The movement was founded to turn the attention of Indian people toward a renewal of traditional spirituality in order to reverse what it believes to be ruinous government policies. AIM has repeatedly brought successful lawsuits against the federal government for the protection of the rights of native nations guaranteed in treaties, sovereignty, and the Constitution. AIM's Web site makes available press releases about many issues of concern to American Indians, including protests against Indian sports mascots, rejection of the Columbus Day holiday, and other issues.

Bureau of Indian Affairs (BIA)
1849 C St. NW, #4160, Washington, DC 20240
(202) 208-7581
Web site: www.doi.gov/bureau-indian-affairs.html

The BIA is responsible for the administration and management of 55.7 million acres of land held in trust by the United States for American Indians, Indian tribes, and Alaska Natives. There are 562 federally recognized tribal governments in the United States. Developing forest lands, leasing assets on these lands, directing agricultural programs, protecting water and land rights, and economic development are all part of the agency's responsibility. In addition, the Bureau of Indian Affairs provides education services to approximately forty-eight thousand Indian students.

The Center for Responsive Politics
1101 Fourteenth St. NW, Suite 1030, Washington, DC 20005-5635
(202) 857-0044 • fax: (202) 857-7809
e-mail: info@crp.org • Web site: www.opensecrets.org

The Center for Responsive Politics is a nonpartisan, nonprofit research group based in Washington, D.C., that tracks money in politics and its effect on elections and public policy. The center conducts computer-based research on campaign-finance issues for the news media, academics, activists, and the public at large. The center's work is aimed at creating a more educated voter, an involved citizenry, and a more responsive government. The report *Indian Gaming Money and Political Influence* is among many generated by the center.

Gam-Anon International Service Office
PO Box 157, Whitestone, NY 11357
(718) 352-1671 • fax: (718) 746-2571
e-mail: info3@gam-anon.org • Web site: www.gam-anon.org

Gam-Anon is meant to help the spouses, families, and close friends of compulsive gamblers. Gam-Anon's purpose is threefold: to learn acceptance and understanding of the gambling illness, to use the program and its problem-solving suggestions as aids in rebuilding lives, and to give assistance to those who suffer from compulsive gambling. The group's Web site offers books, brochures, publications, and fliers concerning gambling problems, recovery, and other issues.

Gambling with the Good Life
4317 S. 179th St., Omaha, NE 68135
(402) 398-3377
e-mail: dhazuka@msn.com
Web site: www.gamblingwiththegoodlife.com

Gambling with the Good Life is a grassroots citizen-action organization dedicated to preserving the good life in Nebraska by opposing expanded gambling in the state. Its Web site has links to many editorials, articles, and reports that discuss the impact casinos have on local businesses, bankruptcies, and other issues meant to mobilize religious and community leaders and others who oppose gambling.

Legi\X Company
1305 Rio Grande Blvd. NW, Albuquerque, NM 87104-2632
(505) 244-4177 • fax: (505) 256-5177
e-mail: info@legix.com • Web site: www.legix.com

Legi\X Company is a lobbying firm that offers an extensive range of services in the areas of political and legislative advocacy, consulting, and fund-raising for tribes, tribal agencies, and other entities. The company provides regular, detailed updates on important issues in the courts, Congress, and the administration, as well as at the state level, concerning tribal sovereignty issues, Indian gaming, economic development, education, and law enforcement.

Midwest Treaty Network (MTN)
PO Box 1045, Eau Claire, WI 54702
(715) 833-8552
e-mail: mtn@igc.org • Web site: www.treatyland.com

The Midwest Treaty Network was founded in 1989 as an alliance of Indian and non-Indian groups supporting Native American sovereignty in the western Great Lakes region. The MTN is working with numerous tribes and tribal organizations throughout the region on issues of cultural respect (such as sacred site protection), opposition to stereotypes (such as Indian mascots), support for environmental protection and land claims, and building cultural and economic ties between native and nonnative communities. The MTN has carried out public educational campaigns with written brochures, research reports, Web pages, an extensive e-mail list, press releases, petitions, legislative testimony, and documentation.

National Congress of American Indians (NCAI)
1301 Connecticut Ave. NW, Suite 200, Washington, DC 20036
(202), 466-7767 • fax: (202) 466-7797
e-mail: ncai@ncai.org • Web site: www.ncai.org

The National Congress of American Indians was founded in 1944 and is the oldest and largest tribal government organization in the United States. NCAI works with its membership of over 250 tribal governments from every region of the country to formulate policy concerning sovereignty, gaming issues, law enforcement, environmental protection, emergency response, education, health care, and basic infrastructure. NCAI's mission is to inform the public and the federal government on tribal self-government, treaty rights, and a broad range of federal policy issues affecting tribal governments. Its Web site offers a tribal directory as well as reports concerning Native American governance, human resources, community resources, natural resources, and other issues.

National Council on Problem Gambling (NCPG)
208 G St. NE, Washington, DC 20002
(202) 547-9204 • fax: (202) 547-9206
e-mail: ncpg@ncpgambling.org • Web site: www.ncpgambling.org

The National Council on Problem Gambling is neither for nor against legalized gambling. The council provides programs and services to assist problem gamblers and their families. The mission of the NCPG is to increase public awareness of pathological gambling, ensure the widespread availability of treatment for problem gamblers and their families, and to encourage research and programs for prevention and education. The council operates the National Problem Gambling Helpline Network; holds conferences; distributes literature on problem-gambling treatment, research, and recovery; and organizes National Problem Gambling Awareness Week. The group offers many books for sale, including *Women Who Gamble Too Much*, *Problem and Pathological Gambling in America*, and *Releasing Guilt About Gambling*.

National Indian Gaming Association (NIGA)
224 Second St. SE, Washington, DC 20003
(202) 7546-7711 • fax: (202) 546-1755
Web site: www.indiangaming.org

The National Indian Gaming Association, established in 1985, is a nonprofit organization of 168 Indian nations engaged in tribal gaming enterprises around the country. The mission of NIGA is to protect and preserve the general welfare of tribes striving for self-sufficiency through gaming enterprises. To fulfill its mission NIGA works with the federal government to develop sound policies and practices and to provide technical assistance and advocacy on gaming-related issues. In addition, NIGA seeks to maintain and protect Indian sovereign governmental authority. Publications include Indian gaming history fact sheets, the *Indian Gaming Resource Directory*, and reports such as *National Survey of Problem Gambling Programs, Gambling in California: An Overview*, and the *Gambling Impact and Behavior Study*.

National Indian Gaming Commission
1441 L St. NW, Suite 9100, Washington, DC 20005
(202) 632-7003 • fax: (202) 632-7066
e-mail: info@nigc.gov. • Web site: www.nigc.gov

The National Indian Gaming Commission is an agency of the United States government established by the Indian Gaming Regulatory Act of 1988 to regulate Indian gaming. The commission publishes Indian gaming fact sheets on its Web site that list gaming tribes, annual revenues, related laws, and other information.

Native American Rights Fund (NARF)
1506 Broadway, Boulder, CO 80302
(303) 447-8780 • fax: (303) 443-7776
Web site: http://narf.org

The Native American Rights Fund is a nonprofit organization that provides legal representation and technical assistance to Indian tribes, organizations, and individuals nationwide. The mission of NARF is to preserve tribal sovereignty, protect tribal natural resources, promote Native American human rights, and develop Indian law. NARF publishes annual reports, press releases, and newsletters concerning Native American legal issues, including those concerned with Indian gaming.

Stand Up for California
c/o Cheryl Schmit, PO Box 355, Penryn, CA 95663
(916) 663-3207
e-mail: schmit@quiknet.com • Web site: www.standupca.org

Stand Up for California is an anti-casino organization formed by community groups, local elected representatives, members of law enforcement, and individual supporters who are directly affected by Indian gaming and tribal sovereignty issues. Stand Up for California hosts and assists with both state and national conferences, debates, and rallies to educate lawmakers and the voting public. Members have testified before local government boards, regional agencies, and state and national commissions about the negative impacts of Indian casinos on communities. The group actively lobbies against bills that expand the scope and intensity of gambling without comprehensive regulation, which may interfere with the civil rights or property rights of citizens in deference to tribal sovereignty. The group's Web site offers reports such as *Casino Impacts and Schools, Gallup Poll on Gambling in America*, and *The Impact of IGRA on Gambling in the U.S. and the Role for State and Local Governments*.

Bibliography

Books

Megan M. Atkinson — *Gambling in California: An Overview.* Sacramento: LAO, 1998.

Thomas Barker — *Jokers Wild: Legalized Gambling in the Twenty-First Century.* Westport, CT: Praeger, 2000.

Brad A. Bays, ed. — *The Tribes and the States: Geographies of Intergovernmental Interaction.* Lanham, MD: Rowman & Littlefield, 2002.

Jeff Benedict — *Without Reservation: The Making of America's Most Powerful Indian Tribe and the World's Largest Casino.* New York: HarperCollins, 2000.

William C. Canby — *American Indian Law in a Nutshell.* St. Paul, MN: Thomson/West, 2004.

Eve Darian-Smith — *New Capitalists: Law, Politics, and Identity Surrounding Casino Gaming on Native American Land.* Belmont, CA: Thomson/Wadsworth, 2004.

Roger Dunstan — *Indian Casinos in California.* Sacramento: California State Library, California Research Bureau, 1998.

Kim Isaac Eisler — *Revenge of the Pequots: How a Small Native American Tribe Created the World's Most Profitable Casino.* New York: Simon & Schuster, 2001.

Kathryn Gabriel — *Gambler Way: Indian Gaming in Mythology, History, and Archaeology in North America.* Boulder, CO: Johnson, 1996.

Rick Hornung — *One Nation Under the Gun.* New York: Pantheon, 1991.

Bruce E. Johansen — *Debating Democracy: Native American Legacy of Freedom.* Santa Fe, NM: Clear Light, 1998.

Ambrose Lane — *Return of the Buffalo: The Story Behind America's Indian Gaming Explosion.* Westport, CT: Bergin & Garvey, 1995.

Oren Lyons, ed. — *Exiled in the Land of the Free: Democracy, Indian Nations, and the U.S. Constitution.* Santa Fe, NM: Clear Light, 1992.

Dale W. Mason — *Indian Gaming: Tribal Sovereignty and American Politics.* Norman: University of Oklahoma Press, 2000.

Carter Jones Meyer, ed.
Selling the Indian: Commercializing and Appropriating American Indian Cultures. Tucson: University of Arizona Press, 2001.

John M. Meyer, ed.
American Indians and U.S. Politics: A Companion Reader. Westport, CT: Praeger, 2002.

Mark Edwin Miller
Forgotten Tribes: Unrecognized Indians and the Federal Acknowledgment Process. Lincoln: University of Nebraska Press, 2004.

National Gambling Impact Study Commission
Final Report. Washington, DC: National Gambling Impact and Policy Commission, 1999.

Paul Pasquaretta
Gambling and Survival in Native North America. Tucson: University of Arizona Press, 2003.

David J. Valley and Diana Lindsay
Jackpot Trail: Indian Gaming in Southern California. San Diego, CA: Sunbelt, 2003.

Jack Weatherford
Native Roots: How the Indians Enriched America. New York: Crown, 1991.

Bill Wright
The Texas Kickapoo: Keepers of Tradition. El Paso: Texas Western Press, 1996.

Periodicals

Chet Barfield
"Indian Casinos' Payout to State Spurs Debate," *San Diego Union-Tribune*, October 10, 2004.

Donald L. Barlett and James B. Steele
"Wheel of Misfortune: The Many Loopholes in the Indian Gaming Regulatory Act of 1988," *Time*, December 16, 2002.

Donald L. Barlett and James B. Steele
"Who Gets the Money? Needy Native Americans, You'd Think. But Indian Casinos are Making Millions for Their Investors and Providing Little to the Poor," *Time*, December 16, 2002.

Michael Beebe
"Casino Deal Principal Admits Ties to Organized Crime," *Buffalo News*, October 15, 2003.

Elaine Bellucci
"Leave Indian Money Alone," *Californian*, May 12, 2004.

John M. Broder
"Deal Is Near on Casinos in California," *New York Times*, June 17, 2004.

Maura J. Casey
"The Hidden Costs of Casinos," *Buffalo News*, October 19, 2003.

David DeVoss
"Heap Big Casinos in Residential Neighborhoods," *Weekly Standard*, September 15, 2003.

Fred Dickey
"Who's Watching the Casinos?" *Los Angeles Times*, February 16, 2003.

William R. Eadington
"The Fallout from Indian Gaming," *California Journal*, September 2001.

Mark Fogarty | "Boom Times for Indian Casinos, Says Merrill Lynch," *Indian Country Today*, July 10, 2003.

John Fund | "Indian Givers," *Wall Street Journal*, September 24, 2003.

Jan Golab | "Arnold Schwarzenegger Girds for Indian War," *American Enterprise*, January/February 2004.

Suzan Shown Harjo | "A History of Critics Getting Our Story Wrong," *Indian Country Today*, March 3, 2003.

Cragg Hines | "The Huge Political Jackpot in Indian Gaming Ventures," *Houston Chronicle*, October 13, 2004.

Chris Ison | "Gambling's Toll in Minnesota," *Reader's Digest*, April 1996.

John W. Kennedy | "The New Gambling Goliath: Christian Activists Struggle to Slow the Rapid Growth of Indian Casinos," *Christianity Today*, August 2004.

David Lazarus | "Greed Tars Indian Casinos," *San Francisco Chronicle*, July 31, 2002.

James May | "An Interview with San Pasqual Chairman Allen Lawson," *Indian Country Today*, June 4, 2003.

Max C. Mazzetta | "State Is Unfair in Taxing Tribes' Casinos," *North (San Diego) County Times*, April 28, 2004.

David Melmer | "Shakopee Mdewakanton Build a Fire Department," *Indian Country Today*, April 22, 2003.

Joel Millman | "Big Chief Pataki," *Wall Street Journal*, March 1, 2002.

Sean Paige | "Gambling on the Future," *Insight on the News*, December 22, 1997.

Christopher Palmeri | "How Casinos Are Hogging the Chips," *Business Week*, October 13, 2003.

Tim Poor | "1 in 5 of Homeless in Survey Blame Gambling," *St. Louis Post-Dispatch*, March 1998.

Ken Silverstein | "Cashing In: Who Makes Money off Casinos on Native American Reservations?" *Nation*, July 6, 1998.

Ernie Stevens | "Tribes Already Sharing with States," *Providence (R.I.) Journal*, February 21, 2004.

Tom Wanamaker | "A Look at Gaming from Another Perspective," *Indian Country Today*, June 5, 2002.

Index